Pahaska Tepee

Buffalo Bill's old hunting lodge and hotel, a history, 1901-1946

• W. Hudson Kensel •

Copyright ©1987 by Buffalo Bill Historical Center

All rights reserved, including the right to reproduce
this book or any parts thereof, in any form, except for
the inclusion of brief quotations in a review.

Library of Congress Catalog Card Number 86-71791
ISBN 0-931618-23-1

Published by Buffalo Bill Historical Center,
P.O. Box 1000, Cody, Wyoming 82414

Design and cover: DD Dowden
Publishing Consultant:
Falcon Press Publishing Co., Inc.
Helena and Billings, Montana

Contents

Acknowledgements

William F. "Buffalo Bill" Cody's exploits as a western plainsman and as an internationally famous showman have been depicted at length in a number of biographical studies. Scholars have given less attention, however, to Cody's activities as a business investor and promoter. Hence, there is little published information dealing with his various business enterprises. This is particularly true of Pahaska Tepee, Buffalo Bill's hunting lodge and hotel, which is barely mentioned in the extensive Cody literature.

Newspapers published in Cody, Wyoming, between 1901 and 1946 proved to be the most valuable sources for tracing Pahaska's history. County courthouse records, government documents and interviews with key people supplied important additional information as well as corroboration for newspaper data. Detailed business records of Pahaska's operation for the period of this study were not available; hence only the surface aspects of Pahaska's financial history could be supplied. Visits to Cody, Wyoming, during the summers of 1981, 1982, and 1984 provided important clues to understanding Pahaska's past.

I wish to acknowledge the help of the late Fred H. Garlow, grandson of Buffalo Bill, who willingly shared with me his knowledge of events at Pahaska over many years and started me on the road to understanding its history. Fred generously supplied me with several rare early photographs from his personal collection and in other ways assisted my research.

I am particularly grateful to Clytie Williams, a Pahaska employee from 1927 to 1937, who made a substantive contribution to Pahaska's history by her sharp recollection of activities there during the 1930s. Clytie arranged interviews for me with local Cody people who had knowledge of Pahaska and in a multitude of other ways facilitated my search.

Merna C. Miller of Twentynine Palms, California, provided valuable insights into the personality and activities of her former father-in-law, Roscoe F. Warren; Mrs. Alice F. Donnell of Worland,

Wyoming, graciously supplied me with a photograph of her parents, Jack and Emma Files, and her impression of life at Pahaska during their period of management; Mrs. Edith Baker Kemp of Basin, Wyoming, gave me many photographs of Pahaska in the early 1930s and her recollections of Pahaska as an employee of that era.

My sister, Gloria P. Lindstrom of Ellensburg, Washington, who shares with me poignant memories of our early childhood at Pahaska, read the manuscript critically and saved me from error at several points. She supplied me with several photographs and helped with the selection of others.

A number of people in Cody, Wyoming, contributed generously in various ways to my research. They include S. P. Van Arsdall, Hugh Brown, Hulda Borron, Grace Craig, Lucille Nichols Hicks, Francis T. Hayden, the late Grace Files Larson, Bill De Maris, Melvin C. McGee, A. R. "Brownie" Newton, Sam Osborne, Ray Prante, Jack Richard, Barbara E. Smith, and Tom F. Trimmer.

Outside of the Cody country, help was given by Horace M. Albright, Jessie F. Alston, Leatha Braden, Aubrey L. Haines, Edwin L. Hall, John E. Jessup, Jennifer D. Kensel, Carl W. Madsen, Sheila W. Olason, Richard C. Overton, Diane Rivera-Pasillas, Don Russell, Dr. Ephraim K. Smith, Merle Spencer, and Leo Urban.

Acknowledgements of help are also due to the directors and librarians of many museums, libraries, historical societies, and government offices. These include Paul Fees, Curator of the Buffalo Bill Museum; Albert C. Minnick, Librarian/Archivist of the Buffalo Bill Historical Center; Valerie Black, Librarian of the Yellowstone Library and Museum Association; Andrea I. Paul, Curator, Nebraska State Historical Society; State Historical Society of Missouri; Ronald J. Mahoney, Associate Librarian and Head, Department of Special Collections and Erland L. Jacobsen, Associate Librarian, Government Publications Department, California State University, Fresno; Kansas City Public Library; Park County Library; Wyoming State Archives Museums and Historical Department; University of Washington Library; Marion W. Pierce, Deputy County Clerk, County of Park, Cody, Wyoming; Forest Supervisor, Shoshone National Forest; Department of Records, Jackson County Courthouse, Kansas City, Missouri; and the Grand Lodge A.F. and A.M. of Missouri, Columbia, Missouri.

Thanks are due to Darrina Turner Damico for her permission to use microfilmed materials on the Lincoln Land Company in the Nebraska State Historical Society and for the use of other information about this company in her possession.

My heaviest obligations are to my mother, Jessie B. Kensel, for her constructive advice and information, and for her abiding love, interest, and support. I am grateful to my son Brendon for his patient and enthusiastic companionship on my trips to Cody and Pahaska, and to my wife Carol who has always given unfailing support to any project I have undertaken.

W. Hudson Kensel

Foreword

It is an honor and a pleasure for me to add a few words to this splendid book, *Pahaska Tepee, Buffalo Bill's Old Hunting Lodge and Hotel*, written by W. Hudson Kensel.

My grandfather, Colonel William F. Cody, better known as Buffalo Bill, traveled extensively in the United States and Europe with his Wild West show. Before the turn of the century he acquired the TE Ranch near Cody, Wyoming, where he spent a great deal of time resting up from his strenuous tours. In 1902 he built a fine large hotel in Cody which he named after my mother, Irma Cody, who was his youngest daughter. Somewhat later he built a beautiful hunting lodge which he called Pahaska Tepee, the Sioux name for "Long Hair's Lodge." Pahaska was located about sixty miles west of Cody near Yellowstone Park. Grandfather loved Pahaska, and it was here that he entertained old friends and members of European royalty by taking them on hunting trips into the beautiful Absaroka Mountains.

During that period our family, consisting of my mother, Irma Cody Garlow; my father, Fred H. Garlow; my brother Bill, sister Jane and myself were living on Buffalo Bill's Scout's Rest Ranch in North Platte, Nebraska, which my parents operated. Grandfather decided to sell Scout's Rest Ranch, and since he needed someone to manage the Irma Hotel, Pahaska and several ranches in the Cody area, my family moved to Cody in April 1913 to take over the management of these various enterprises.

We spent our winters in Cody and our summers at Pahaska Tepee. Reading Hudson's book brought back fond memories of the summers I spent at Pahaska, fishing in the nearby North Fork River and riding and hunting in the surrounding mountains. I killed my first elk about five miles above Pahaska Lodge.

I well remember the large lobby in the lodge with its tremendously large fireplace made out of native boulders. Guests would gather in the evening around the blazing logs in the fireplace, listening to the old player piano, or dancing and singing until bedtime.

One of my first jobs, when I was about twelve years old, was being a bellhop at Pahaska. I recall trying to wrangle two suitcases at once while tramping up the narrow staircase to the lodge rooms upstairs. Old homemade pole beds, the water pitchers and wash bowls on the washstands with commodes underneath, will always live in my memory.

This interesting and accurate history of Pahaska that Hudson has written is based on extensive and careful research. Those of us who have the privilege of reading this book will always remember and love Pahaska Tepee.

Fred H. Garlow
Grandson of Buffalo Bill
Cody, Wyoming

(Note: This was written by Fred Garlow, grandson of W. F. Cody and trustee of the Buffalo Bill Memorial Association, shortly before his death on June 21, 1985. Mr. Garlow knew Pahaska and the surrounding mountains as few have been privileged to, from the days of his grandfather through the ownership of his friends, the Henry H. R. Coe family.)

Introduction

This is a history of Pahaska Tepee, a hunting lodge and hotel which Col. William F. "Buffalo Bill" Cody built near the eastern boundary of Yellowstone National Park. The story begins in 1901 when Col. Cody selected the site for Pahaska and ends in 1946 when Alberta E. Wilkinson sold Pahaska to Henry H.R. Coe. That year was an important benchmark in Pahaska's history because it marked the beginning of an extensive modernization program which in many ways altered Pahaska's original character.

The central theme of this study is the evolution of Pahaska as a mountain resort. Col. Cody used it as a hunting lodge, but it had a greater importance to him as a business. He constructed a triumvirate of hotels—Pahaska, the Irma Hotel, and Wapiti Inn—to provide accommodations for tourists brought to the town of Cody, Wyoming, by the Burlington Railroad. His ultimate objective in building these hotels went beyond personal gain to his desire to do everything necessary to promote the growth and commercial development of Cody. These hotels enhanced the prospects of Cody as a starting point for Yellowstone National Park by establishing convenient stopping places for tourists—the Irma in Cody, the Wapiti Inn, and Pahaska, located thirty-six and sixty-two miles respectively from Cody on the road to the east entrance.

Soon after Col. Cody's death in 1917, Pahaska was sold by the Cody estate, and thereafter it passed through the hands of a succession of owners down to 1946. This study analyzes these changes in ownership and the accompanying expansion of Pahaska's physical facilities and services.

Since Pahaska was built in a mountain wilderness this study is also concerned with those developments which offset the disadvantages of isolation and allowed Pahaska to become a successful business operation. These include the building of the Cody Road between Cody, Wyoming, and Yellowstone National Park and the development of transportation systems to carry tourists to the park.

Despite its isolation, Pahaska's location was unique and advantageous. To the west lay Yellowstone National Park whose scenic wonders would in time attract millions of visitors. To the east lay Cody, Wyoming, connected by the Burlington Railroad and by highways to the population centers of the Midwest and East. Thus, the completion of the Cody Road provided the essential link which gave Pahaska access to hordes of tourists. Situated in a magnificent setting and favored by its association with the internationally known Buffalo Bill, Pahaska itself was a destination worthy of travelers, as well as others who stopped briefly for meals and lodging en route to Yellowstone National Park.

The development of the means for transporting tourists from Cody to Yellowstone National Park would also profoundly affect Pahaska's future as a mountain resort. Tex Holm's and Charles Marston's horse-drawn coaches and wagons carried the first tourists through the east entrance into Yellowstone. In time, horses and coaches were replaced by the privately-owned automobiles and the yellow buses of the Yellowstone Park Transportation Company. The efficiency of these improving transportation systems was reflected in the expansion of Pahaska's tourist facilities.

Finally, this study is concerned with the many roles Cody citizens played directly or indirectly in fostering Pahaska's growth. Over a period of many years, the Cody Club donated money and local people volunteered their equipment and labor for the construction and repair of the Cody Road. In addition, Cody's business and professional people loyally attended the annual "Grand Openings" of the tourist season at Pahaska. Newspaper accounts of these festivities and complimentary descriptions of Pahaska helped to popularize it as a recreational center for local people.

1 | Pahaska's Beginnings

The first passenger train of the Chicago, Burlington and Quincy Railroad rolled into the little town of Cody, Wyoming, on the morning of November 13, 1901. The usual dignitaries present on ceremonial occasions were aboard, but the presence there of the colorful Col. William F. "Buffalo Bill" Cody gave the event a special significance. Buffalo Bill was returning to Cody that fall to rest after another arduous tour with his famous Wild West show. With him on the train was an entourage of friends, including the Reverend George Allen Beecher, pastor of the Episcopal Church of North Platte, Nebraska; Mike Russell of Deadwood, South Dakota; two Indians, Black Fox and Iron Tail, and others who had been invited to join Col. Cody on a big game hunt.

A procession was formed on the arrival of the train and a large Concord coach drawn by six horses carried the distinguished party into town. After a greeting by Mayor Frank L. Houx, the train party and every cowboy within a radius of 100 miles marched around town led by a brass band. Fireworks and a wild game barbecue finished the celebration of the historic entrance of the new line of the Burlington Railroad.[1]

After the festivities Col. Cody and his party left for his TE Ranch located some thirty-five miles from Cody on the South Fork of the Shoshone River. There the party was outfitted for the westward trek into the mountains. Col. Cody asked Walter A. Kepford, pioneer South Fork rancher and experienced guide, to lead the party up the North Fork of the Shoshone River. Charles Hartung also joined the group as a guide along with Ed Robinson who doubled as guide and trip photographer. John "Reckless" Davies, boon companion of the Colonel, came along as general handyman, and Billy Burns was the horse wrangler.

Both Walter Kepford and the Reverend George Beecher wrote accounts of their experiences of this hunting expedition. According to Kepford, the large party rode up the North Fork trail and set up a permanent camp about a mile below the confluence of the North

Fork and its major tributary, Middle Creek. The hunting party spent nearly two weeks in the area and managed to bring down five deer, three elk, and a brown bear. Ed Robinson took a photograph of the assembled party and their wild game at the permanent camp. Later, the artist Irving R. Bacon painted a large picture from this photograph. This oil painting now hangs in the Buffalo Bill Historical Center in Cody.[2]

In his autobiography, the Reverend Beecher also had included his account of the hunting trip and his version of how Pahaska Tepee was named. He relates that one day Col. Cody halted the hunting party on the promontory that lies to the west of where Middle Creek flows into North Fork. There Cody expressed his hope that a road would soon be built through this place connecting the town of Cody to Yellowstone National Park. Six years earlier the colonel had scouted the North Fork Valley and had followed Middle Fork up to Sylvan Pass. He had determined then in 1895 that this was the best route for an east entrance road. Now, in 1901, with the town of Cody a reality and its rail connection completed, Col. Cody was confident that the government would soon complete an east entrance road. Congress had appropriated funds for the road in 1900, and by 1901, surveying and construction was underway. At the time of this November 1901 hunting expedition, Col. Cody's good friend, Theodore Roosevelt, had been in the White House just two months, and the colonel felt he could count on the President's support in securing the necessary congressional appropriations to finish the road. Cody then told Beecher and the rest of the hunters gathered there that he planned to build a hunting lodge at this very place. According to Beecher's account, Cody then took a hand ax and blazed several trees to mark the location of the lodge. He turned to Beecher and said, "Mr. Beecher, I propose that we call the inn, 'Beecher Inn,' in your honor as our guest on this hunting trip." The colonel then turned to interpret this information to Iron Tail who suggested that Pahaska or Paha-Haska, the colonel's Sioux Indian name, was a better choice. Beecher graciously agreed to this at once. This apparently is the origin of the naming of Cody's lodge in the Absarokas—Pahaska Tepee—translated from the Sioux language as Long Hair's Lodge.[3]

The reminiscences of Kepford and Beecher provide conclusive evidence that Col. Cody chose the site of Pahaska in 1901. There is, however, less certainty about the year when construction on the lodge began. Memoirs, reminiscences, newspaper accounts, and various documentary and historical materials relating to the Cody country give few hints as to the precise year in which the lodge was built. Those that do almost always cite 1901 as the construction date. This is clearly a year or two too early.

The Wyoming Stockgrower and Farmer published in Cody during the early 1900s is remarkably silent on the subject of Pahaska in its weekly issues for 1902 and 1903 when construction of the lodge must have commenced. Col. Cody spent very little time in the Cody country in any given year, since most of the time he was on tour with his Wild West show. When he did make his annual appearances in Cody in the late fall or winter, his goings and comings and all his local activities were reported in the newspaper in copious detail. Numerous newspaper articles discussed his various ranches, his investments in local mines, his involvement with the Cody Canal, and his irrigation schemes for the Big Horn Basin. He was the social leader of Cody and its primary investor and promoter. Literally everything he did and said was grist for the local newspaper mill.

Thus it seems inconsistent that there are no accounts of Pahaska while it was being built—none until July 5, 1904, when its formal opening was announced. The construction of Pahaska was possibly started in 1902, but it seems more likely that work was begun in 1903. The opening of the Cody Road to the east entrance of Yellowstone National Park on July 10, 1903 would have greatly facilitated the transportation of building materials to the construction site. Lodgepole pines were in abundance at the site for use in the main framework of the lodge, but hardware, roofing materials, and sawn lumber would have had to be hauled up the North Fork Valley from Cody in freight wagons. Moreover, the Irma Hotel in Cody was under construction between August 1901 and November 1902 at a cost of $60,000-$80,000. Col. Cody's major interest in 1902 was the completion of the Irma and quite possibly he didn't have the funds that year to begin another major project.[4]

A newspaper editorial listing Col. Cody's investments at or near Cody covering the period between March 1, 1901 and December 1, 1902 included the Cody irrigation canal, four ranches, Buffalo Bill Barn, Irma Hotel, a brickyard at Cody and other investments and expenditures which totaled $216,500.[5] There was, however, no listing of expenditures for Pahaska. A newspaper article in August 1903 reporting the trip of Cheyenne photographer J. E. Stimson up the Cody Road and into Yellowstone National Park contains no mention of Pahaska. A construction project just underway would have understandably evoked no comment, but a lodge as imposing as Pahaska situated right on the road could hardly have been overlooked by a professional photographer. Another party which also left Cody in August 1903 for a trip through the park included a Reverend J.D. Cain. Cain's detailed observations on this trip also contain no hint of a large lodge beside the road—although most certainly Cain observed some construction work in progress.[6]

Abraham Archibald Anderson designed Pahaska Tepee for Col. Cody sometime during 1902 or 1903. That the two men were on friendly terms is well documented in Cody's letters to his sister Julia Goodman and in Anderson's autobiography.[7] There are no known accounts of discussions between Cody and Anderson on the subject of drawing plans for Pahaska, but early newspaper accounts and statements of early Cody residents testify to the fact that Anderson did design Pahaska.[8]

About 1886 A. A. Anderson came from New York to Wyoming. He liked the state so well that he founded the Palette Ranch on the Greybull River near the town of Meeteetse. Anderson, who was an avid hunter, soon became an ardent conservationist when he concluded that bands of sheep allowed to graze freely in the public forests would not only destroy the forests but also their wildlife, which he loved to hunt. He was distraught to see smoke rising from the burning forests lying to the west of his ranch. Anderson surmised that these fires were accidentally or deliberately caused by out-of-state sheepmen who moved their flocks across the public forests. Anderson visited President Roosevelt in Washington, D.C. in 1901 and urged him to enlarge the existing forest reserves around Yellowstone National Park. Roosevelt was persuaded, and in 1902 by executive order created an enlarged Teton and Yellowstone Forest Reserves which lay respectively to the south and east of the park. Roosevelt then appointed Anderson Superintendent of the Reserves.[9]

Anderson was much more than a rancher and forest administrator. Born in 1847 in New Jersey to upper middle class parents, Anderson was educated at the Columbia Grammar School and under private tutors in Europe. Having demonstrated artistic talent, he studied art in Paris and emerged as a noted water color artist and portrait painter. He married Elizabeth Milbank, who had inherited a multi-million dollar fortune from her father, a railroad director.[10] Thus, never troubled with financial worries, Anderson painted as he wished, traveled internationally and hobnobbed with heads of state and with the wealthy upper crust of America and Europe. Haughty, aristocratic and self-righteous as he was, Anderson also possessed a rare combination of many talents, was enormously knowledgeable in diverse fields and had the drive and energy to achieve his life's aims.

Col. Cody was extremely fortunate to have the gifted Anderson design his hunting lodge. Anderson's experience as an architect was limited, but he had designed the notable Beaux Arts Building in New York City and his own Palette Ranch lodge. Anderson's forte was that, as a wealthy man who mingled with the rich and famous around the world, he could well understand Cody's requirements in a lodge which would be visited by that same set of notables. Though there were enormous differences between the two men in education, temperament, and style, they also shared certain values and characteristics that gave them a common ground. Both men were cosmopolitans, but loved the West above all places on earth. Both were ardent outdoorsmen and hunters and built lodges in which to entertain their friends from around the world. Both men were in perpetual motion, and though they had little time in which to develop a close friendship, each respected the other.

Cody had always demonstrated great pride in the edifices which he constructed. His Scout's Rest Ranch in North Platte, Nebraska was planned as the show place of western Nebraska, with a palatial house and the biggest barns in the country.[11] He lavished a great deal of effort and money and a beloved daughter's name on his Irma Hotel, and bragged, with some justification, that it was the best-equipped hotel in the state of Wyoming.[12] Cody selected a mountain site of unusual beauty for his hunting lodge, and as Pahaska rose on the landscape, it too reflected his pride and attention to detail. A. A. Anderson, with the soul of a western man and the fine perceptions of an artist, embodied the ideal architect for Pahaska.

On a flat bench just above the mixing waters of the North Fork and Middle Creek, a site was cleared among the towering lodgepole pines. Here, at 6,672 feet in the Absaroka Mountains, the construction of a two-story lodge was begun. Pahaska Tepee, facing the morning sun, rose unobtrusively in the little valley at the foot of Sylvan Pass. Here in the understated rustic elegance of Pahaska the hunter and traveler alike would find the ideal retreat from life's cares and draw inspiration from the bright flowers, rushing streams, and tall pines of the surrounding mountains. Here at Pahaska, far from the burdens and trials of the Wild West show, Cody could do the things he enjoyed most—entertain his friends and feel the freedom of his beloved mountains. It was, as he said many times, the "Gem of the Rockies."[13]

On July 5, 1904, the Cody newspaper announced the grand opening of "Buffalo Bill's Middle Fork Inn," the uninformed editor's version of the new Pahaska Tepee. Col. Cody wasn't present for this occasion, but four months later he arrived in Cody with a large party of friends.

Col. William F. "Buffalo Bill" Cody on the south porch of Pahaska Lodge sometime during this first hunting trip there, November 5-15, 1904. The absence of the porch roof and porch rails indicate that the lodge was still unfinished. Photo courtesy Fred H. Garlow, Cody, Wyoming.

The hunting party, including a pack train, cook and guides, arrived at Pahaska on November 5 for a ten-day hunt. The party included several wealthy Englishmen, Major General Nelson A. Miles, Dr. Frank Powell, Major John Burke, Iron Tail, and Cody's twelve-year-old nephew, Walter Goodman, the son of his sister Julia Goodman. A painting of this assembled group in front of the not-quite completed Pahaska was made from a photograph by R. Farrington Elwell in 1904. Another photograph on the same occasion shows Cody standing on the unfinished south porch of the lodge.

Deer, elk and bear were plentiful around Pahaska and this first hunting party was successful, with young Walter bagging his first elk and the others bringing in their share of meat and heads for trophies.[14]

Pahaska was, of course, to be the fall hunting lodge of Cody, but the colonel from the first also saw the place as a stopping point for tourists on the wagon road from the town of Cody to Yellowstone National Park. Wapiti Inn, located near the junction of Elk Fork Creek and the North Fork River about thirty miles from Cody, was conceived and built by the colonel at the same time Pahaska was going up as the first stopping point for tourists en route to the park. As

early as 1905, when construction was still going on at both Wapiti
Inn and Pahaska, they were advertised as Buffalo Bill's rustic inns
in the Rockies. Cody envisioned a growing volume of tourists coming
to the town of Cody over the new Burlington line. He expected that
they would spend money in various Cody businesses—including
his Irma Hotel—and then proceed up the Cody Road by easy stages,
stopping for lunch at Wapiti Inn and then for supper and lodging
at Pahaska before going up Sylvan Pass to the park.[15]

Col. Cody was a born optimist and promoter, and a man of
vision who did his best to grasp the main chance. Occasionally his
vision was faulty and his business judgment failed—and sometimes
his friends or advisors led him into financial sinkholes. But in the
matter of envisioning the agricultural possibilities of the Big Horn
Basin and in promoting the town of Cody as the jumping-off point
to Yellowstone National Park, he did not fail.

Col. Cody enjoyed a warm friendship with Charles E. Perkins,
President of the Chicago, Burlington and Quincy Railroad (1881-1901),
and was a guest on many occasions on the train magnate's private
railroad car. There is little question that this close relationship helped
to expedite the Chicago, Burlington and Quincy's construction of
a 131-mile branch from Toluca, Montana to Cody in 1901—thus giving
Cody and the Big Horn Basin a valuable transcontinental connection. Perkins was a shrewd, hardheaded man who would never make
business decisions based on sentiment. Unquestionably, however,
Cody's enthusiasm and his ability to articulate his vision helped to
convince Perkins of the value of railway access to Yellowstone
National Park, and more important, to the potentially productive
Big Horn Basin.[16]

Col. Cody made certain he had taken all the necessary steps
to get this railroad connection. About forty years earlier he and a
partner had located a townsite along the Kansas-Pacific Railroad's
projected route across Kansas. The partners refused to sell an interest
in the townsite to the railroad when it was requested, and as a con-
sequence the railroad located another town, Hays City, not far away.
Cody's dream of wealth vanished, and he determined not to make
that kind of mistake again.[17] In 1901 not only did Cody have the
support of his friend Perkins, but he and his partners in the townsite
of Cody agreed to give the Lincoln Land Company, a subsidiary of
the Burlington Railroad, one-half of the lots in the new town of Cody.
In addition, it has been alleged that Col. Cody promised Alfred
Hymer (sometimes spelled Heimer), a Lincoln Land Company
official, that he would build hotels along the route to the park so

that the tourists Burlington transported to Cody would have proper accommodations. Col. Cody may initially have made such a promise because he was willing to do almost anything to ensure a railroad connection. It is difficult to believe that this promise, if it was actually made, could have had any impact on Cody's decision to build Pahaska or, in fact, even on the railroad's decision to build to the town of Cody. Tapping the Big Horn Basin's agricultural productivity was the railroad's prime objective in building to Cody. Carrying tourists to the park would generate some additional source of revenue for the railroad, but this certainly was an insufficient justification for building an expensive branch line into Cody.

Moreover, Hymer, a minor official of the Lincoln Land Company, would not have had the authority to have bound either Col. Cody or the railroad to the fulfillment of certain conditions to guarantee the railroad's entrance into Cody. Neither in the published autobiography of Charles H. Morrill, President of the Lincoln Land Company, or in the extensive papers relating to the operations of this company in Cody—which are stored in the Nebraska Historical Society—is there any mention of Col. Cody's being obligated to build hotels along the park route.[18]

Col. Cody did not build Wapiti Inn and Pahaska to accommodate the railroad; he built them to accommodate his own interests, which were to promote and develop the Cody Road to the park thus enhancing the success of his namesake city. And not incidentally, of course, Col. Cody intended to use Pahaska as the base for his occasional fall hunting trips into the Absarokas.

It would be difficult to document from newspapers and other sources that Col. Cody visited Pahaska more than six times between his first hunt there in 1904 and the time of his death in early 1917. The primary use of the lodge from the beginning was as a hotel for tourists, rather than as the colonel's private hunting lodge. Pahaska was a business. Col. Cody expected to make money there, just as he did at Wapiti Inn and Irma Hotel. Newspaper advertisements were soon proclaiming the benefits of staying at "Buffalo Bill's Hotels in the Rockies."[19]

2 | The Cody Road

The development of Pahaska as a profitable mountain resort was dependent upon a complex of factors. The railroad connection to Cody and the Cody Road to the park were established just prior to the completion of Pahaska. Beyond these basic requirements was the need to constantly improve the Cody Road and the mode of transporting tourists over it. The improvement of roads, hotels, camps, and transportation systems in Yellowstone National Park to make it a national tourist attraction would have significant bearing on Pahaska's economic health. The advertising campaigns of the Burlington Railroad, the state of Wyoming, and the city of Cody to attract tourists to the park's east entrance would be important to Pahaska. Finally, the ultimate advertisement for Pahaska Tepee was that it was Buffalo Bill's old hunting lodge. Down to the present it is this fact and the legends that it has inspired that have given Pahaska its special distinction.

The Cody Road built from the town of Cody up along the winding North Fork River, past Pahaska and into Yellowstone National Park, was the product of many hands. The Corps of Engineers, United States Army; the United States Reclamation Service; Big Horn County; and the people of the town of Cody all made important contributions to the construction of the road.

In 1895 Col. Cody had ridden up the North Fork Trail and determined that Sylvan Pass was the easiest approach to the park. Later he contacted Wyoming's Representative Frank W. Mondell (member of the United States Congress, 1894-96; 1898-1922) and got his support for an appropriation to build an east road into Yellowstone National Park. By the Sundry Civil Act of June 6, 1900, Congress authorized construction of a wagon road from the outlet of Yellowstone Lake to the eastern boundary of the Yellowstone Timber Reserve, which became Shoshone National Forest in 1907. This act provided for an initial appropriation of $20,000 to build the road and the necessary bridges. Captain Hiram M. Chittenden of the Corps of Engineers, United States Army, was the officer in charge of the work of constructing and maintaining roads and bridges in Yellowstone National Park. It was under his guiding genius that the road system in the park was completed between 1899 and 1906. One of his subordinates, S. F. Crecelius, Assistant Engineer, was in direct charge of locating and building the east road.[1]

On June 30, 1901, Crecelius reported that reconnaissances on the Absaroka Range, which extends along the east boundary of the park, revealed that Jones, Crow and Sylvan passes were practicable crossings. Sylvan Pass was finally adopted because at 8,500 feet above sea level it was still 1,000 feet lower than the other two passes. Once this decision was made, the work of location and construction was begun on July 5, 1901. Among the bridge sites chosen was one over the North Fork of the Shoshone River just above the mouth of Middle Creek—very near to where Pahaska Tepee would be built.[2]

Road construction continued through the summer of 1901, 1902 and 1903 on this fifty-six mile route from the northern tip of Yellowstone Lake to the eastern boundary of the Yellowstone Forest Reserve. In his annual report to the Chief of Engineers in 1903 it is interesting to note that Captain Chittenden had serious reservations about the eastern approach to the park ever becoming an important tourist route because of the late melting of snow in Sylvan Pass. Another of his failures in prophesy was that the use of automobiles in the park could never be adopted because of the danger of frightening the teams of horses which pulled wagons and coaches into and around the park.[3]

On July 10, 1903, the east road, or Cody Road, as it came to be known, was officially opened to traffic, although repairs and improvements went on annually throughout the following summers to make the road safer for travel. Among the chief priorities in this regard was the widening of the road in Sylvan Pass, which was too narrow for safe passage. The east road was essentially complete in 1905 with the construction of a viaduct, later called the Loop or Corkscrew Bridge, by which the road down the mountain on the east side of Sylvan Pass was made to pass over itself in order to reduce the extreme gradient.[4]

Meanwhile, the people of Cody recognized that their future as an outfitting center and starting point for the park lay in the completion of a good wagon road up the North Fork. An important link to this potentially lucrative tourist business had been completed in 1901 when the Burlington Railroad entered the town. Another link was being forged that same year with construction of a new government road underway from the park to the eastern boundary of the forest reserve. The third and final link would be to complete a forty-mile road from the town of Cody to meet the government road coming from the west.

By December, 1901, a subscription paper for the road was being held at the bank of Amoretti, Parks and Company. Cody people were urged to call and sign the paper—presumably to pledge a certain amount of financial support. Felix Alston, a contractor, had agreed to complete the road by July 1, 1902, at a cost of $1,000.[5] A year later, *The Wyoming Stockgrower and Farmer* called upon the commissioners of Big Horn County to assist in the building of the road to the full extent of the county's ability and to be liberal in their appropriations for the new road.[6]

Some manner of road was completed by 1903, but it is apparent that it was far from satisfactory. One newspaper commentator observed, "If the people of Cody don't want this route condemned by the traveling public, they will have to get a hustle on and fix that part which connects this town with the new government road."[7] Still another report noted:

> A. Holms, who recently returned from the park, says that the government road across the forest reserve is a dandy, and that the county road between Cody and the reserve line would be fine if the boulders were thrown out of the track.[8]

The Reverend J. D. Cain observed in a newspaper account describing his trip between Cody and the park that "The county road should be put in better repairs to make the first day's drive a pleasant one."[9] The Cody Commercial Club responded to these criticisms by voting to add $50.00 to the $150.00 already appropriated by the county that year for repair work.[10]

A description of travel over this segment of the Cody Road was given in 1936 by Dave Jones, an early Cody businessman:

> It was a hot August day in 1905 when the squeaking, grinding, rattling caravan of chuck wagons, surreys and buckboards, carrying eighteen happy individuals, wound its way out of Buffalo Bill's home town to tour nature's wonderland, Yellowstone Park. The caravan forded Sulphur Creek at the present bridge site on the Park road, then traveled over the bench east of Cedar mountain thru Indian Pass, then close by the south side of the mountain down into Poverty Flat, crossing the Southfork close to what is now the center of Shoshone Reservoir, then over

the bench passing by the then Trimmer, Marston, and Martin ranches that now lie at the bottom of the lake, chugging and bouncing along over what was little more than a cow trail.[11]

The route of this rather primitive county road was soon to change. In 1903 the Reclamation Service of the United States began studying the feasibility of storing water above Shoshone Canyon where there was a good reservoir site. These studies demonstrated the practicability of such a plan and the Shoshone Project was organized for the purpose of providing water for the irrigation of a large area in the vicinity of Cody. The plan was to store the water in a large reservoir formed by building the Shoshone Dam in the gorge of Shoshone River between Rattlesnake and Cedar mountains.[12] A project office was established in Cody and the preliminary work got underway. Since construction materials would have to be hauled from Cody to the dam site, work on a wagon road from the mouth of the canyon to the cliffs above the elevation of the dam was begun in 1904 and finished in 1905. For the greater part of the four mile distance the road was cut into the solid rock of the canyons.

The old road to the park, which went around Cedar Mountain, would be flooded out when the reservoir was filled, so it became imperative to continue the completed canyon road westward. Harry W. Thurston, Supervisor of Shoshone National Forest from 1907 to 1911, took the initiative to do this. In 1908 he learned that the Secretary of the Interior, James R. Garfield; F. H. Newell, Chief Engineer of the U.S. Reclamation Service; and Congressman Nicholas Longworth and his wife Alice Roosevelt Longworth were visiting Yellowstone National Park. Thurston contacted the distinguished group and urged them to investigate the road project from the canyon to the national forest. Thurston met them at Pahaska and escorted the party down the tortuous route to the canyon. The officials realized the urgent need and the result was authorization of the funds for the Reclamation Service to build a road from the canyon to the Kelly (now Wapiti) Bridge, provided the county would build the seven-mile stretch from there to the national forest. Soon thereafter, A. C. Newton, chairman of the board of Big Horn County Commissioners, announced that the board had accepted the arrangement unanimously. These two connecting links were begun in 1908 and finished in 1910.[14] As a result of this great improvement in the Cody Road, the number of people entering the park by the East Entrance jumped from 767 in 1910 to 1,524 in 1911.[15] This favorable change in statistics would have a positive effect on Pahaska, then emerging as a popular stopping-off point for tourists as well as local people, whose primary destination was the lodge, where they would spend a few days or a few weeks relaxing and enjoying its marvelous scenery and good fishing.

In 1909 Calvin W. Williams, the Wyoming state immigration agent, and his touring companion Edwin Hall, the state geologist, drove their E.M.F. Studebaker up the Cody Road during a 3,500-mile trip around the state. Thirty years later Williams wrote his account of the journey and gives us this observation about the Cody Road in 1909:

> West of Cody, going to Yellowstone Park, we found the best road in the state. It was intentional and not an accident. It followed the Shoshone Canyon and we followed it to the Park entrance, looking up on one side and down on the other. However, it was not as wide as it might have been or no doubt is today; nor was it hard-surfaced; yet it gave us something to talk about in an un-profane way.[16]

3 | Buffalo Bill's Hotel In The Rockies

In the spring of 1905 work on Pahaska Tepee and Wapiti Inn was nearing completion, and the town of Cody, population 1,220, waited expectantly for the crowds of people it hoped would come to visit Yellowstone National Park. The Burlington Railroad advertised the daily arrival, except on Sunday, of No. 311 and the daily departure, except for Saturday, of No. 312. Sleeping, dining and reclining cars were provided on all through trains, and Pullman sleeping cars ran between Cody and Toluca, Montana. The arriving tourists would find excellent accommodations in Cody's new luxury hotel, the Irma, as well as in the Hart Mountain Inn and the Cody Hotel and in various boarding houses around town. On May 31 the newspaper reported that Cody guides and outfitters had nearly 200 parties booked for the beautiful trip up the North Fork to the park.[1]

At the turn of the century there were several means by which tourists from Cody could visit the park. Those with enough confidence and experience could simply go alone on horseback with a pack outfit. A better way for those who wanted to go to the park independently would be to form a party of genial people and hire a guide, cook and horse wrangler to assume the responsibilities and work of the trip. Those independent parties were accountable to no one but themselves, could set their own time schedule, take whatever route they chose, and venture out on as many sidetrips as their nerve and food supply would permit.

Another method for traveling to the park was for tourists to join a party that was being organized by a local guide and accept the limitations imposed by his established schedule and tour route. It was difficult to establish from available data just exactly who was the first guide to take tourists into Yellowstone National Park from Cody, but Aron "Tex" Holm was certainly among the first who did. Until 1903 there were vehicular entrances into the park only from the north, south and west. From these points wagon roads connected into the present figure eight loop which encircles the central part of the park.

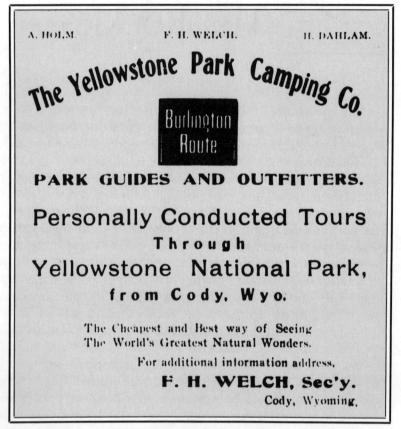

Figure 1: This advertisement appeared in The Wyoming Stockgrower and Farmer *during the summer of 1905.*

In 1900, Tex Holm and his wife left Cody with two saddle horses and a buckboard and went up Sylvan Pass to Old Faithful, Mammoth and finally to Cooke City, Montana. This experimental trip convinced Holm that tourists could be conducted into the park from the east despite the lack of a road. In 1901 Tex and Mrs. Holm, with a young wrangler and four couples from Chicago, left Cody on horseback. They took along a wagon with a roundup box behind and a spring wagon in case someone got tired of riding horseback. This trip was in reverse of the direction taken by the Holms the previous year. The party spent two difficult weeks going over Dead Indian Hill, up the Clark's Fork and Crandall Creek to Cooke City. From there they went over the mountains to Mammoth, around Old Faithful and back to Cody by way of Sylvan Pass. In his memoirs Holm recalls that "It was a pretty fair trail, then, to Sylvan and over the pass." But at one point the party encountered a ledge so narrow that the wagons had to be unloaded and carried across by hand with the help of a government construction crew that was then at work building the Cody Road. As they left the park the Holm party followed the North Fork, fording it four times, and at the site of the old Marquette settlement now covered by the Buffalo Bill Reservoir, they forded the South Fork and returned to Cody.

Other early local guides who took tourists into the park from Cody were Charles Marston and the Barron Brothers of Marquette and Walter Braten of Cody. Somewhat later Nedward Frost and Fred Richard, the Dahlem Brothers, and L. W. Nordquist and C. H. James of the Shoshone Camping Company would provide guide services.[2]

The tours organized by these guides followed a specific route according to a predetermined schedule. In 1905 Tex Holm and two partners organized the Yellowstone Park Camping Company (fig. 1). The new company advertised two classes of trips to the park—one of fifteen days duration, the other of twenty-one days. The advertisement noted that:

> With each party we furnish four-horse mess or supply wagons, the necessary number of specially constructed covered, three-seated mountain hacks, canvas floored tents (accommodating two people each), good beds, mess and cook tents, guides, cooks, drivers, etc.[3]

The Holm-conducted party would leave Cody the morning of the first day, passing through the proposed reservoir of the Shoshone Irrigation Project and up the North Fork as far as Wapiti. The journey would continue the second day up the picturesque North Fork road, arriving at the east entrance of Yellowstone by evening. From there the party would travel up Sylvan Pass into the park, viewing Yellowstone Lake, the geyser basin, the Grand Canyon of the Yellowstone, and other points of interest before returning down Sylvan Pass and back to Cody.[4] Tourists who entered the park by the east entrance as independents or with guides like Tex Holm and Frost and Richard numbered 310 in 1903; 313 in 1904; 403 in 1905; 808 in 1906; 545 in 1907; 762 in 1908; 805 in 1909; and 808 in 1910.[5]

The independent groups which came up the Cody Road after 1904 would probably have been more likely than the organized ones to stop at Pahaska for supplies, food or lodging. However, the Cody newspaper would report from time to time that guided parties paused at Pahaska. One lady from Austin, Illinois, stated in a newspaper account of her trip into Yellowstone National Park in 1909 with Tex Holm that she danced at Pahaska on her way in and again on the way out of the park.[6] In 1910 Tex Holm obtained a permit from the Forest Service and built Holm Lodge on Libby Creek, some seven miles east of Pahaska. With this new facility the Holm parties had less need than ever of stopping at Pahaska.[7]

Pahaska was formally opened as a hotel for tourists in 1905, but no advertisements were carried in the newspaper announcing this. Articles mentioned that both Pahaska and Wapiti Inn offered accommodations to the traveler, but they also noted that carpentry work was still in progress at both places under the supervision of Dr. Frank Powell.[8]

In February 1906, May Bradford, Col. Cody's sister, arrived in Cody to take charge of Cody's local interests. The following month Louis E. Decker also appeared in Cody. Decker, Col. Cody's trusted associate in the Wild West show, was to share managerial duties with the widowed Mrs. Bradford. A romance developed and before the year was over, on December 23, the two were married.[9]

The first advertisement for "Pahaska Inn" appeared in *The Wyoming Stockgrower and Farmer* on June 14, 1906, along with the Irma and Wapiti Hotel as "Buffalo Bill's Hotels in the Rockies." Similar ads appearing in 1907 corrected these names to "Pahaska Tepee and Wapiti Inn" (figs. 2 and 3). W. F. Cody was listed as proprietor and L. E. Decker as manager. Newspaper advertising of the accommodations available at Pahaska continued fairly consistently every week for the next ten years.

As noted earlier, the annual reports of the Superintendent of Yellowstone National Park show that the number of people entering the park from the east entrance ranged from 310 to 808 in the years 1903-1910. This trickle of tourists, traveling for the most part with organized tours, would not ordinarily have stopped at Pahaska—though some did. Local news columns of Cody newspapers regularly carried items about various individuals or families who were spending a week or two or perhaps all summer at Pahaska. The advertised rates were $3.00 per day and $15.00 weekly for rooms in the lodge. By 1911 bathing facilities were provided in a cabin located immediately to the right of the lodge. Meals were cooked on a big wood range in the lodge kitchen situated in a room just off the south end of the dining room. Food was served on large tables in the long dining room which ran nearly the full width of the lodge just behind the living room. Later the wood range was moved into the dining room and placed to the rear of the huge stone fireplace— its stovepipe connecting directly into the fireplace chimney.

Four two-room log cabins, newly constructed in 1909, were arranged in a gentle arc to the left rear of the lodge facing southeast and south. They were completely furnished for light housekeeping and were rented for $5.00 a week. A fifth log cabin, smaller than the others and located between them and the lodge, displayed a large sign with the word "STORE" running the full length of the front roof line. Guests renting the cabins or passing tourists could buy provisions there. Horses available for rental at $1.00 a day rounded out the services offered by early Pahaska.[10]

Managers Louis and May Decker were in charge of all three of Col. Cody's hotels, and the newspaper regularly reported their visits to Pahaska. The resident manager of Pahaska from 1906 to 1911 was Major E. S. Hoopes. A veteran of the Spanish American War, he had actually been discharged as a corporal but he was popularly accorded the rank of major because he always wore a distinguished Vandyke beard. Hoopes lived at Pahaska the year round, acting as caretaker during the winter months. Talented with the violin, Hoopes was often called upon to fiddle at local barn dances and at the numerous dances held at Pahaska.[11]

Col. Cody's hunting trips to Pahaska never interfered with the tourist business of the lodge, because he arrived there in November or December at the conclusion of the yearly tour of the Wild West show. At that time Yellowstone National Park had closed and cold weather had discouraged tourist traffic. Moreover, the colonel's visits to Pahaska were infrequent. The TE Ranch, located on the South Fork River about thirty-five miles southwest of Cody, Wyoming, was his regular winter headquarters. From there his hunting parties ranged over the mountain country around the North and South Fork rivers. The few times he hunted out of Pahaska seem to have been reserved

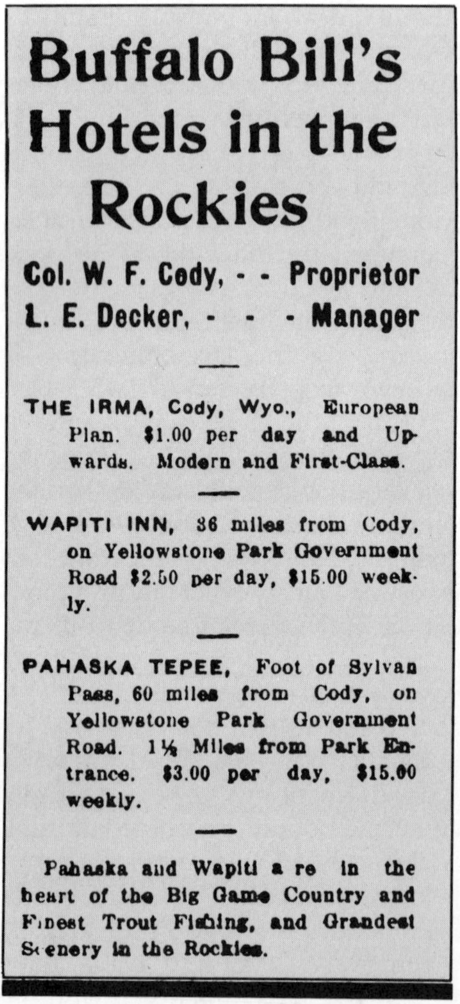

Buffalo Bill's Hotels in the Rockies

Col. W. F. Cody, - - Proprietor

L. E. Decker, - - - Manager

THE IRMA, Cody, Wyo., European Plan. $1.00 per day and Upwards. Modern and First-Class.

WAPITI INN, 36 miles from Cody, on Yellowstone Park Government Road $2.50 per day, $15.00 weekly.

PAHASKA TEPEE, Foot of Sylvan Pass, 60 miles from Cody, on Yellowstone Park Government Road. 1½ Miles from Park Entrance. $3.00 per day, $15.00 weekly.

Pahaska and Wapiti are in the heart of the Big Game Country and Finest Trout Fishing, and Grandest Scenery in the Rockies.

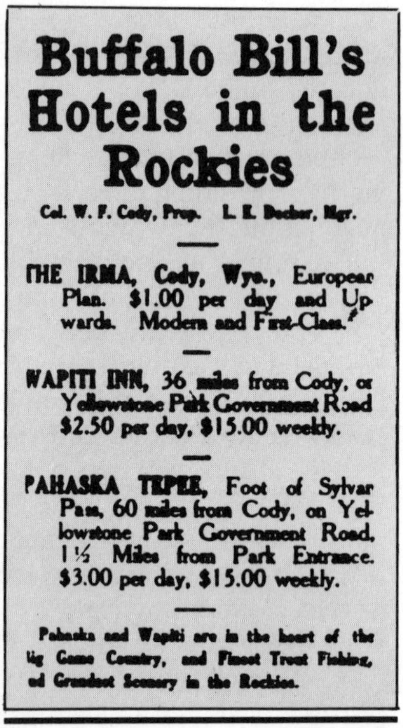

Buffalo Bill's Hotels in the Rockies

Col. W. F. Cody, Prop.   L. E. Decker, Mgr.

THE IRMA, Cody, Wyo., European Plan. $1.00 per day and Upwards. Modern and First-Class.

WAPITI INN, 36 miles from Cody, or Yellowstone Park Government Road $2.50 per day, $15.00 weekly.

PAHASKA TEPEE, Foot of Sylvan Pass, 60 miles from Cody, on Yellowstone Park Government Road. 1½ Miles from Park Entrance. $3.00 per day, $15.00 weekly.

Pahaska and Wapiti are in the heart of the Big Game Country, and Finest Trout Fishing, and Grandest Scenery in the Rockies.

Figure 2: This advertisement first appeared in The Wyoming Stockgrower and Farmer *in the summer of 1907 and ran in consecutive issues until April 23, 1913. At that time Louis E. Decker was replaced as manager by Fred H. Garlow and the latter's name began to appear in the advertisement.*

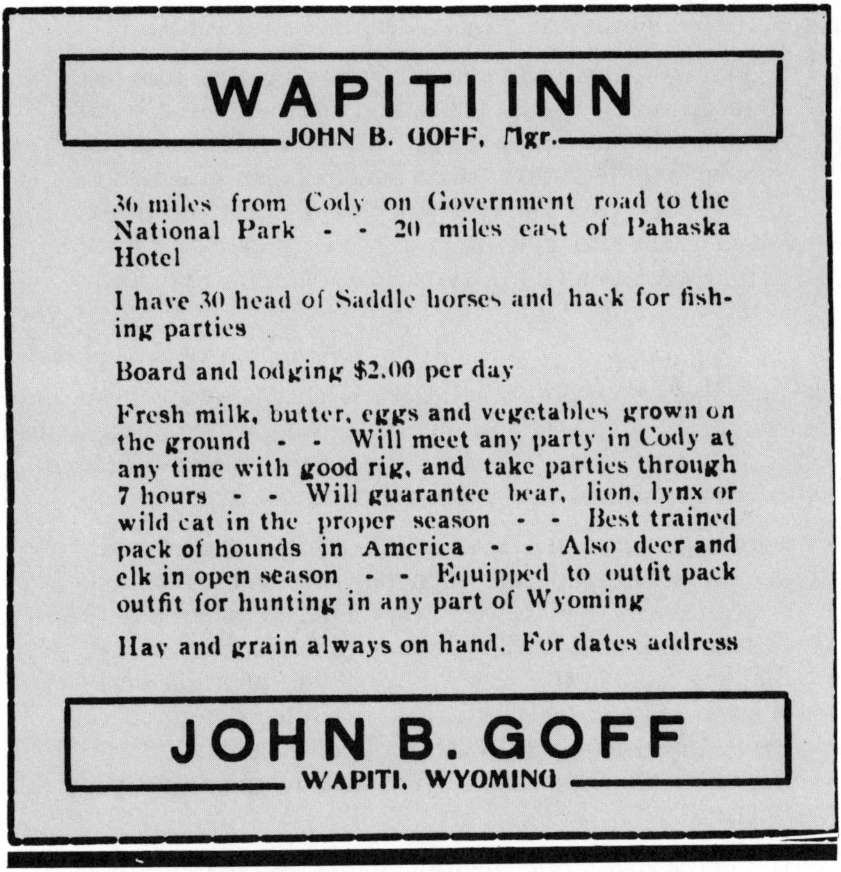

WAPITI INN
JOHN B. GOFF, Mgr.

36 miles from Cody on Government road to the National Park - - 20 miles east of Pahaska Hotel

I have 30 head of Saddle horses and hack for fishing parties

Board and lodging $2.00 per day

Fresh milk, butter, eggs and vegetables grown on the ground - - Will meet any party in Cody at any time with good rig, and take parties through 7 hours - - Will guarantee bear, lion, lynx or wild cat in the proper season - - Best trained pack of hounds in America - - Also deer and elk in open season - - Equipped to outfit pack outfit for hunting in any part of Wyoming

Hay and grain always on hand. For dates address

JOHN B. GOFF
WAPITI, WYOMING

Figure 3: This advertisement appeared in The Wyoming Stockgrower and Farmer *during the summer of 1908.*

for special guests or for those occasions when he really needed rest and to be alone in the companionship of his closest friends.

His first hunt at Pahaska was in 1904, the second in 1908. His remarks to his partner, Major Gordon Lillie, in 1909 as their show season was ending reveals Cody's deep need for Pahaska:

> You know, Major, by the time the season closes, I am just about all in. The constant noise and turmoil, both day and night, wears on a fellow. I can hardly wait till I reach my hunting lodge (Pahaska). I take a bunch of congenial friends, a good cook, and plenty of good stuff to eat and drink. We go up there to hunt, play cards, relax and rest for three or four weeks, and it brings back my old self—Billy Cody again.[12]

Cody's hunting party at Pahaska in 1909 included his old friend Mike Russell of Deadwood, South Dakota; Jake M. Schwoob; Mr. and Mrs. George T. Beck; Mr. and Mrs. S. A. Watkins; and Mrs. Louis Decker, all of Cody. John "Reckless" Davies, the colonel's old friend, was the chief guide. A newspaper article noted that:

> Prior to the erection of the beautiful Pahaska hotel, the parties camped out, but since then they have had all the modern conveniences in the very heart of the big game country and the great dining hall, with roaring fireplace at one end, the long table in the center, loaded with juicy elk steak, venison roast and bighorn stew, reminded the guests of scenes presented by Sir Walter Scott in his famous descriptions of the hunting parties of the ancient barons of Merry England.[13]

The newspaper commented on another modern convenience when it observed that Jake Schwoob drove the hunting party down from Pahaska with his automobile up to its hubs in slush and mud. The success of the machine in plowing through everything seemed to be the final test as to the practicability of its use in the locality.[14] In fact, earlier, on June 4, 1909, *The Wyoming Stockgrower and Farmer* carried a large advertisement stating that a White Steamer automobile would begin to make regular trips between Cody and Pahaska. This advertisement proved to be one year premature.

The year 1910 heralded the beginnings of Pahaska's heyday as a mountain resort. The Shoshone Dam-Reservoir segment of the Cody Road was completed, shaving several miles off the distance between Cody and Pahaska and providing a better roadway. This narrow, winding dirt road full of chuckholes and dotted with occasional boulders from cliffs above, bore no resemblance to the modern highway there today. But to the people of Cody in 1910 the road was a boulevard compared to the rough trail that had been there earlier.

Col. Cody intended in 1909 to put a sixty horsepower White Steamer automobile into service carrying tourists from Cody to Wapiti Inn and to Pahaska. The auto failed to arrive that year, but the *Park County Enterprise* announced that the new White Steamer had been shipped on June 27, 1910, from Cleveland, Ohio, and was expected shortly. The driver-engineer, Jack Winter, who had already arrived in Cody, was employed by Cody as his principal driver from 1910 to 1912. When Winter resigned in August, 1912, he was replaced by A. G. Deckerhoff.[15]

The Irma Hotel, Wapiti Inn and Pahaska were to be operated on a greater scale than ever, with the new White Steamer making regularly scheduled trips to the mountain resorts. The automobile made its first regular trip to Pahaska on July 5, 1910. The charge for a round trip was $5.00. The Steamer left the Irma every Tuesday and Thursday at 9:00 A.M., reaching Wapiti Inn for lunch and arriving at Pahaska at 3:00 P.M.

On Saturdays the auto left the Irma at 2:00 P.M. and arrived at Pahaska for supper (fig. 4). On Saturday, July 16, the White Steamer left the Irma at 2:10 P.M. carrying a load of 1,800 pounds to Pahaska, arriving there by 6:30 P.M. Returning the next morning in a heavy rain storm, Jack Winter put chains on the car and plowed through the mud to Cody only thirty minutes off-schedule and in plenty of time to meet the train. These feats seemed to demonstrate that the Steamer was the right auto for use on the Cody Road. The White Steamer schedules were, of course, coordinated with the arrival and departure of the Burlington train. By the beginning of the 1911 tourist season two more White Steamers had been added to the Cody-Wapiti-Pahaska run.[16]

Manager Louis Decker added a number of improvements to Pahaska in anticipation of an increased number of tourists. Among these was a log laundry house which he built near the bank of the North Fork, about fifty yards to the right of the lodge. A large wood range was installed there for heating water and hand irons. Later a gas-heated mangle for ironing the hotel linen completed the furnishings. In succeeding years the gas mangle produced considerable excitement and concern over the fires it caused in the laundry house. Decker announced that a new bathhouse was being built and that

Hunters Attention

Buffalo Bill's Hotels in the Rockies

Pahaska

60 miles from Cody, on the Yellowstone Park Road, is in the very heart of the

Big Game Country

Best of accommodations for man and beast. Rates $3.00 per day, $15.00 per week, open till Dec. 1. An ideal headquarters for hunters. Big game season opens Sep. 25, closes Nov. 30. White steamer automobiles transport passengers from Irma Hotel, Cody to Pahaska and return at $5.00 round trip. White steamer express carries baggage at reasonable rates. You can hunt out from hotel and will not require expensive camp and pack outfits, cooks, horses wranglers, etc. Make your accommodations now.

Address

L. E. Decker, Mgr.

Mgr. Irma Hotel, Cody, Wyo.

To Pahaska

by Palace Auto

An Ideal Outing at very moderate expense...

The Palace White Steamer leaves the Irma every Tuesday and Thursday at 9 a.m., reaching Wapiti for dinner, and arriving at Pahaska at 3 p.m., return trips Wednesdays and Fridays.

Sunday Outing Trip

On Saturdays the auto leaves the Irma at 2 p.m., after arrival of train from the east, arriving at Pahaska in time for supper. The return trip Monday morning, is made in time to connect with the east bound train, thus enabling traveling men to spend Sunday at Pahaska and lose no time.

FARE Cody to Pahaska and return, $5; Cody to Wapiti and return, $4.

RATES Wapiti, $2.50 per day or $15 per week; Pahaska, $3 per day or $15 per week; furnished 1-room log cabins, complete for housekeeping, $5 per week. Supplies may be purchased from our store room at Pahaska.

Tickets on sale at the Irma.

L. E. Decker, Mgr.

CODY, WYOMING

Figure 4: This advertisement, above, appeared in the Park County Enterprise *first on July 20, 1910, and throughout the rest of the summer of 1910.*

Figure 5: The advertisement at left, appeared in the Park County Enterprise *from August through November, 1910.*

an electric lighting system was being installed in the lodge. Water for the first time was to be piped directly to the lodge from a nearby mountain stream. The newspaper reported that Pahaska was enjoying a phenomenal popularity, with fifty-eight people staying at the hotel on Sunday, July 24, 1910. Manager Decker stated that every log cabin was filled with excursionists and that more cabins were to be erected to the right of the hotel. The Sunday guests included several from out-of-state and a number of Cody people—Mr. and Mrs. George T. Beck, Mr. and Mrs. D. E. Hollister, W. J. Deegan, Jake Schwoob, William Hogg and family, Dr. and Mrs. Bennett, Gus Holm, Ben Rief, Harriet Rossiter, and others.[17]

As summer faded on Pahaska's banner year, the lodge's services for hunters were strongly advertised (fig. 5). Pahaska would remain open for the big game season, which began on September 25th and closed on November 30th. The White Steamer was standing by to transport the hunters and their luggage at reasonable prices. The advertisement pointed out the advantages of Pahaska, where hunters could hunt out of the hotel and wouldn't be required to hire expensive camp and pack outfits, cooks, horses, wranglers, etc. A Pahaska-bound hunting party was reported leaving Cody in four cars on the morning of November 26, 1910. The group, consisting of H. M. Gerrans of Buffalo, New York; the George T. Becks, J. M. Schwoobs, B. C. Rumseys, H. C. Fergusons, L. E. Deckers, and Dexter Rumsey, all of Cody; and Mrs. T. J. Foley of Omaha, stayed at Pahaska until December 7. The feast they enjoyed there was described in detail, but no mention was made of success or failure in hunting.[18]

4 | Competition and Growth, 1910-1912

Holm Lodge, which Tex Holm had built in 1910 seven miles east of Pahaska, was the only mountain resort which offered any competition to Pahaska for a number of years. In its early phase the lodge served primarily as a stopping place for the Holms' tourist parties en route to Yellowstone National Park. The newspaper announcement of its opening on August 6, 1910, did state, however, that Holm Lodge was open to the general pleasure-seeking public. Pahaska's advertisement of August 24, 1910, touting its advantages as a headquarters for hunters was matched on October 1 by Holm Lodge's advertisement for hunters to use quarters at the lodge for the hunting season. Again, as at Pahaska, emphasis was placed on the money to be saved by staying at the lodge where all the necessary horses, pack outfits and guide service could be secured (fig. 6).[1]

In June 1911, Holm purchased two Studebaker E.M.F. automobiles. Each car had a capacity of five persons and made daily trips between Cody and Holm Lodge. These cars apparently weren't satisfactory, because the next year Holm sold them and bought a twelve-passenger Stanley Steamer. It is interesting to note that both Manager Decker of Pahaska and Tex Holm hired crews over a period of years to remove rocks, build bridges and do any other necessary kind of repair work to keep the Cody Road open to their resorts.[2]

In 1911, 1,524 tourists, more than twice the number than in 1910, entered Yellowstone National Park from the East Entrance. Traffic began to crowd Cody Road, still too narrow for two-way traffic. Turnouts were provided where one could wait or back out of the way until the other party had passed. Automobiles were not yet permitted in the park, but an increasing number of them headed for Pahaska or Holm Lodge or for private camps along the North Fork River. The majority of people still went up the Cody Road by horse-drawn wagons or stages and the noise of automobiles often caused the horses to rear and bolt. Despite these difficulties, the advent of the automobile and improved roads meant increasingly heavy tourist traffic in the coming years.[3]

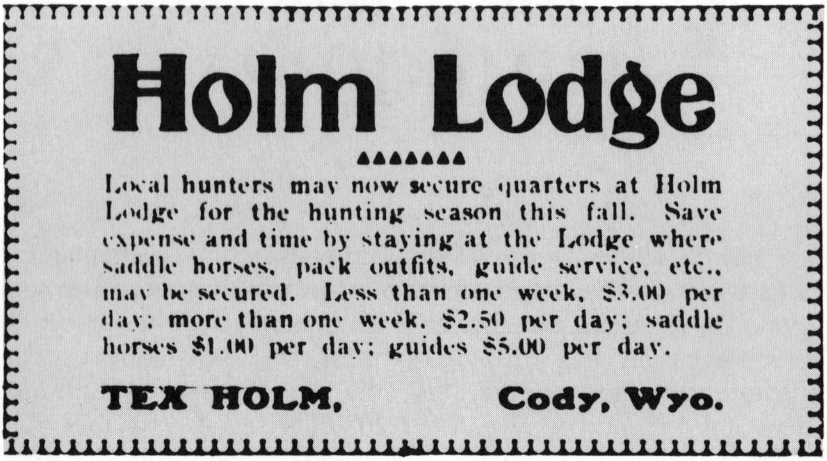

Holm Lodge

▲▲▲▲▲▲▲

Local hunters may now secure quarters at Holm Lodge for the hunting season this fall. Save expense and time by staying at the Lodge where saddle horses, pack outfits, guide service, etc., may be secured. Less than one week, $3.00 per day; more than one week, $2.50 per day; saddle horses $1.00 per day; guides $5.00 per day.

TEX HOLM,   **Cody, Wyo.**

Figure 6: This advertisement appeared in the Park County Enterprise *during the fall of 1910.*

Pahaska opened on June 10, 1911, with a party for Cody notables and many others from the towns and ranches of Park County who motored to the lodge. After a supper feast, the congenial crowd was treated to fireworks on the lodge lawn, which spread out in front of the lodge as far as the bank overlooking the North Fork River. This was followed by singing and dancing until midnight to the accompaniment of Major Hoopes on the fiddle and Mrs. Harry E. Miller on the piano. On the following day the guests explored the grounds and enjoyed the scenery. An interesting description of Pahaska was provided in the newspaper report of this event:

The tepee proper is a large two-story log structure, with the main part occupied by a great living room, two stories in height and having a great stone fireplace as its crowning glory. On the floor are brilliant Navajo blankets, the walls are hung with buffalo hides, while from the rafters of the roof hang the flags of all nations, relics of the Wild West shows. To the right, one enters the dining room, with its walls of unplaned logs and side-board of cut poles.

The living room takes the form of an open gallery at the second floor and opening into the guest chambers of which there are twenty-three. The rooms are wonderfully attractive and in keeping with the general plan. The rough mortised doors are assuredly more appropriate than any product of chisel and plane. Within each room is an iron bed, a rug, a dresser and wash-stand—there is hot water for the asking, don't forget also the bathhouse with its array of six porcelain tubs.[4]

A row of four cabins to the left rear of the lodge provided additional space. In the middle of the row was a spigot providing water, and the small cabin store immediately to the left rear of the lodge sold provisions to the cabin guests. All of the cabins had two rooms and were completely furnished. The article noted that, "There is a little sheet-iron cooking stove in the corner, the china closet with the dishes, pots, pans and skillets already furnished. Then there is a table, a diminutive washstand, a dresser and iron bed."[5]

There were also several tent houses set up to the right and in front of the lodge on the lawn. They were built with a wood floor resting on logs with wood framing three feet above the ground. Army duck provided the rest of the wall and roof. The room inside was twelve by fourteen feet and was furnished with a small heating stove, iron bed, rug, dresser and small washstand. A carriage house was located to the right of the lodge beyond the bath house. This building, originally constructed in 1905, was later enlarged so that it could house automobiles. About one hundred and fifty yards back to the right of the carriage house were a barn and stables.

At some distance up the hill to the right rear of the lodge a huge wooden tank was set on supports as a water supply. It was filled with water from Middle Creek which flowed through a pipe from a point about a half-mile upstream from the lodge. A hydraulic ram kept the pressure constant and a pump provided about 180 gallons of water per hour.[6]

In June, 1911, not long after the opening party, Louis Decker erected a round dancing pavilion directly back of the lodge about two hundred feet. It was fifty feet in diameter with a framework of rustic logs and top of canvas. Seats were built around the inside of the walls. The pavilion was torn down in 1926, but not before many notable dances had been held there.

Opening day, June 10, 1911, at Pahaska. This photo by A.G. Lucier of Powell, Wyoming, shows the assembled weekend guests on the roadside with Pahaska Lodge and cabins in the background. Among the regular visitors to Pahaska were Mr. and Mrs. George T. Beck and daughters Betty and Jane standing by the second car from the left. Seated in the third car from the left are Mr. Jake M. Schwoob in the rear and Mrs. Schwoob at the wheel. Photo courtesy Peg Garlow, Cody, Wyoming.

Decker announced in the same month that a tennis court, rifle range, and croquet grounds were to be laid out at Pahaska, and he invited the public to attend a "Grand Fourth of July Celebration at Pahaska." Fireworks, dancing in the new pavilion, tennis, croquet, and rifle shooting would furnish "A Grand Good Time." Automobile transportation was available at the Irma Hotel with departure at 8:00 A.M. on July 4th (fig. 7).[7]

Later that month the Park County Automobile Association held its annual meeting at Pahaska—a practice that was to continue for a number of years. This association with D. E. Hollister, President; Mrs. Dorothy Trimmer, Vice President; Adam Hogg, Secretary; and W. J. Deegan, Mayor of Cody, the Treasurer, was formed to work for the improvement of the county roads, the making of road maps, and the assistance of auto tourists. After a business meeting at which it was decided to meet again at Pahaska in two weeks, the group enjoyed a dance in the new pavilion. At the second meeting in early August, virtually every

Several Park County Automobile Association members and their friends pose in the new Pahaska Dancing Pavilion during the weekend of their annual meeting, July 15-16, 1911. Resident manager E.S. Hoopes, fiddle in hand, stands near the center of the group. Photo courtesy Buffalo Bill Historical Center, Cody, Wyoming

automobile in Cody made the trip to Pahaska. The dancing pavilion was again the focal point for enjoyment.[8]

In August, 1911, a fourth White Steamer was secured to meet the heavy tourist traffic to Pahaska. It was reported that there were forty people at the lodge with more arriving every day. Large numbers of tourists en route to Yellowstone National Park were also putting strains on the organized tour companies. The Yellowstone Camping and Transportation Company, headed by Tex Holm, conducted eighty-five people into the park in August—the largest tourist party ever handled out of Cody to that date. Later Ned Frost and Fred Richard would conduct parties in excess of 100. To meet the growing demands of their trade, Frost and Richard purchased the 320-acre ranch of H. B. Robertson located on the North Fork, twenty-five miles west of Cody. By shifting the headquarters of their operation from Cody to the new ranch,

Grand Fourth

OF

July Celebration

at **Pahaska**

Fireworks, Dancing in the Pavillion, Tennis Court, Croquet, Rifle Range.

A Grand Good Time

Autos leave Irma Hotel: Tuesday morning, July Fourth, at 8 o'clock

Figure 7: This advertisement appeared in the Park County Enterprise *during June, 1911.*

twenty-five miles closer to Yellowstone National Park, they would lessen the wear and tear on their vehicles and horses and have a place where they could raise alfalfa for the horses. Fred Morris, who had established a dude ranch on the North Fork in 1910, was also enthusiastic about the volume of tourists on the Cody Road in 1911. By early July over thirty eastern guests—called dudes at the time—were staying at his place. The dude ranch business was just getting underway in the Cody area, and Pahaska and Holm Lodge had not long to enjoy their exclusiveness as the only stopping places on the road to Yellowstone National Park.[9]

Pahaska was host to several distinguished visitors during the summer of 1911. Mrs. Charles E. Perkins, wife of the former president of the Burlington Railroad, and a party of friends spent a week there. Wyoming's United States Senator Francis E. Warren spent a night at the lodge en route to the park. Judge Parmelee held a brief court session in Pahaska's dancing pavilion, finishing up the affairs of the Bench Canal Company of Germania. In September, about twenty-five members of the National Press Club visited Pahaska at the conclusion of a three-week tour of Yellowstone National Park. This group, which included representatives of nearly every big-city newspaper, had entered the park through the southern entrance at Jackson's Hole and traveled by mountain wagons through the park, down Sylvan Pass to Pahaska. Nine cars from Cody, owned by Jake M. Schwoob, the Irma Hotel, Bob Rumsey, George T. Beck, Harry Ferguson, Tex Holm, and E. J. Sullivan, were driven to the lodge to meet the tired newspapermen. Dinner was served to fifty-one people in the long dining room behind the massive stone fireplace. The following day, the wagon-sore newspaper delegation enjoyed the luxury of an automobile ride to Cody, where the town fathers took great pains to impress the writers with new developments around town.[10]

By late September the summer cycle moved into its final phase. Tourists returned home, and hunting parties headed for the mountains. Bronson Rumsey of Buffalo, New York, joined H. B. Robertson, George Hamilton, George T. Beck, and Bob Rumsey at Pahaska for a hunting party. One of the men, George T. Beck, had just recently established a new automobile speed record between Pahaska and Cody. With W. T. Hogg as his only passenger, he covered the fifty-six mile distance in a record two hours and twenty-three minutes, stopping only three minutes for water.[11]

Manager Louis Decker announced in June 1912 that Mrs. Myrtle Watkins of Cody would replace Major Hoopes as resident manager of Pahaska. William Cody Boal, the grandson of Col. Cody, was to be assistant manager, and Mrs. John Winter the storekeeper. The grand

EXCURSIONS!

This Saturday and Every Saturday Till the Close of the Season
WEEK END EXCURSIONS TO PAHASKA

A 120 mile ride in the luxurious, easy riding White Steamers over one of the most beautiful scenic roads in the world, to the most charming resort in the Rocky Mountains.

PAHASKA, The Gem of the Rockies.
One Fare ($5.00) for the Round Trip.

Cars leave The Irma Hotel Saturdays at 1 :30 p. m. Returning, leave Pahaska Mondays at 8 a. m., arriving at Cody in time for noon train.

Figure 8: This advertisement appeared in the Park County Enterprise *during the summer of 1912.*

opening of Pahaska was held June 8 with the doors and grounds thrown open to the numerous guests from Cody and other points in Park County. Following the bounteous dinner which was always served at this event, the guests gathered around the fireplace in the living room of the lodge. The rugs were rolled up and the dance began. These "grand openings" were held for the purpose of building good will among Cody people and to bring their attention to new improvements and attractions at Pahaska. Pahaska was heavily advertised in the local newspapers after Decker became manager (fig. 8). He planned several special events every summer to draw people up the Cody Road. On July 13, a huge advertisement appearing in the *Park County Enterprise* proclaimed a barbecue, dance and fireworks at Pahaska. Josh Deane of Meeteetse, a chef of local fame, was to barbecue an ox. The charge for a plate was one dollar and music would be furnished by the Corn Stalk Fiddlers. Pahaska's White Steamer would leave the Irma at 9:00 A.M. Saturday and return to Cody early the following Monday. Bill DeMaris of Cody was twelve years old when his mother drove their Franklin automobile to Pahaska to attend this event. He recalls that the trip took three and one-half hours over a rough, dusty road. Josh Deane had buried a whole beef in the ground, covered it with canvas and cooked the meat three days and three nights. The finished result, DeMaris remembers, was delicious (fig. 9).[12]

The most important addition to Pahaska in 1912 was a fine large log house built by Col. Cody for the use of the Park County Automobile Association. This building, which henceforth was called the Club House, contained two rooms. The largest was used as a lounging and reading room containing chairs, couches and library tables. The smaller of the rooms was used as a kitchen. A large screened porch was built across the front. This new building was located behind the lodge and immediately to the north of the dancing pavilion.[13]

In 1913, Col. Cody asked his daughter Irma and her husband Fred Garlow to take charge of the Irma Hotel, Pahaska and Wapiti Inn. The Garlows arrived in Cody in April and Louis and May Decker, who had been managers since 1906, left for Denver. Col. Cody had asked Decker to take charge of an event called the Last Great Council of the Indians which was to be a part of the Denver Pageant in 1915. In May, Mr. and Mrs. George F. Walliker arrived in Cody from Omaha to replace Mrs. Watkins as resident manager at Pahaska. Mrs. Walliker was Mr. Garlow's sister.[14]

An announcement was made the same month that would give Pahaska's tourist business a considerable boost. In 1911 Tex Holm had merged his Yellowstone Park Camping and Transportation Company

BARBECUE!
Dance and Fireworks at Pahaska
Saturday, July 13

BARBECUE from noon. Dancing in the Pavilion in the evening.
The finest fireworks that ever came to the country, Saturday night.
Ox roast by that old timer, JOSH DEAN, of Meeteetse, and assistants
———— PLATES, $1.00 ————

Music By The Corn Stalk Fiddlers.

Cars leave the Irma at 9 a. m., Saturday. Returning leave Pahaska
at 8:30 a. m., Monday. · · · · $5.00 Round Trip

Figure 9: This advertisement appeared in the Park County Enterprise
during the early weeks of July, 1912.

with the Tex Holm Livery Company to form the Holm Transportation Company. This corporation with its local members, J. M. Schwoob, W. L. Simpson, W. J. Deegan and others, provided additional capital for the enlargement of Holm's successful tour business in the park. Holm's tour camps in 1911 consisted of Holm Lodge, Sylvan Pass Lodge located near Sylvan Lake, and Squaw Lake Camp near the shores of Yellowstone Lake. In 1912 the Secretary of the Interior granted a permit to the corporation to conduct a regular transportation business in the park. This permit was later renewed and extended to 1917. Prior to 1912 Holm had operated with temporary permits which were difficult to obtain and burdened with various restrictions. The permit granted in 1912 allowed the corporation to establish permanent camps within Yellowstone National Park and freed it from earlier restrictions on the number of tourists it could handle, the number of vehicles it could operate in the park, and the route it had to follow in the park. The Holm Corporation responded immediately by enlarging its facilities at Sylvan Lodge and by erecting a number of new buildings at other points in the park: two cabins and a stable at Lake Yellowstone camp; a cabin and stable at West Thumb; two large cabins, a mess house, a bunkhouse and a large stable near Old Faithful geyser; a lunch station, two cabins and a stable at Norris; and at Canyon, two cabins and a stable. Tex Holm spent the winter of 1912-1913 giving illustrated lectures to audiences in cities throughout the East and Middle West portraying the scenic beauty of the Cody Road and the advantages of entering the park along that route. In May 1913, as the Holm Transportation Company braced itself for the expected deluge of tourists, it made an arrangement with Manager Fred H. Garlow that would greatly improve the business prospects of Pahaska. All tourists conducted into and out of the park by Holm Transportation Company were to be guests at Pahaska for their meals and overnight lodging. Holm Lodge was not to be abandoned; the tourist trade was simply to be moved to Pahaska, and Holm Lodge would concentrate on its growing business in providing for summer boarders and vacationists.[15]

The Wylie Permanent Camping Company, which also had a permit to transport tourists through the park and operate permanent camps, opened an office in Cody in 1912 in anticipation of a large volume of tourist traffic. This company had previously conducted tourists into the park only from the northern and western entrances. The Holm Company arranged with the Wylie Company to transport their tourist parties to the East Entrance where the Wylie Company vehicles would pick them up. The Holm and Wylie parties thus were both given meals and lodging at Pahaska en route to the park. By the end of September, the

Club House at Pahaska. This large log house was built behind Pahaska Lodge by Col. Cody in 1912 for use by the members of the Park County Automobile Association. Later it was used for many years as the resident manager's home. Photo courtesy Jessie B. Kensel, Ellensburg, Washington.

Holm Company had transported 500 people to the park over the Cody Road as well as 200 more they had carried to Pahaska for the Wylie Company. Pahaska was an obvious beneficiary of the increased park traffic and the new arrangements the transportation companies had made.[16]

On November 12, 1913, the main building at Holm Lodge was completely destroyed by fire. This event was a severe blow to the Holm Transportation Company, which had been committed since its organization in 1911 to an extensive and costly expansion of its camping facilities in Yellowstone National Park. In addition to the expense for constructing and staffing new buildings at various points in the park in 1912, the Holm Company had also spent $1,000 on horses and purchased three new Stanley Steamers in 1913. The main building at Holm Lodge had had no sleeping rooms, so guests were housed in tent cabins prior to 1912 when four new frame cottages were erected. In 1913, five additional cabins were constructed. These heavy financial outlays undoubtedly influenced the company's decision not to assume the estimated cost of $2,000-$2,500 for rebuilding the main structure at Holm Lodge. Six months later, in May 1914, the cabins, salvaged lodge furniture and the horses of Holm Lodge were sold to J. W. "Billy" Howell and H. Hillis Jordan of Cody. Apparently as a part of its agreement with Howell and Jordan, the Holm Transportation Company then changed the pattern of its previous two years' operation by stopping for food and lodging at Holm Lodge during the summer of 1914 rather than at Pahaska.[17]

5 | A Famous Hunt & Unusual Events, 1913-1914

Pahaska had its grand opening on June 14, 1913, with the usual fanfare: a dinner for fifty guests—with the Becks, the Garlows, the Schwoobs, the Rumseys, the Deegans, the Hollisters, Mrs. William Simpson and children Virginia and Milward, and other loyal Cody people in supportive attendance. Following a bounteous feast the party retired to the dancing pavilion behind the lodge. Music was furnished by Fay Hiscock, Cody's pioneer photographer, and by Bill Barron. When the dancers had exhausted this duo they were relieved by George T. Beck on the piano with Jake Schwoob assisting with a mouth harp. The following day the members of the Park County Automobile Association who were there held a meeting in the new Club House.[1]

In 1913 Wapiti Inn was torn down and the salvaged lumber moved to Pahaska, where it was used in making improvements. Wapiti Inn, located about thirty-six miles up the road from Cody, had been a convenient lunch stop in the days of wagon and coach traffic. However, the advent of the automobile, along with faster speeds made possible by improved roads allowed tourists to reach Pahaska by lunchtime. Wapiti Inn was no longer as functional as it once had been. A Sundry Civil Bill, approved by Congress on August 24, 1912, had provided an initial appropriation for the widening and improvement of entrance roads as well as connecting roads within Yellowstone National Park. Work on widening these roads to eighteen feet began in 1913, and it was clear that it was only a matter of a few years before automobile traffic would be permitted in Yellowstone National Park. This development would lead rapidly to nearly universal use of automobiles by travelers coming up the Cody Road and thus was another factor dooming Wapiti Inn's continued existence.[2]

The salvaged lumber from Wapiti Inn was used in part to build a long bunkhouse structure immediately to the north of the lodge. It contained a number of separate guest compartments which would help to accommodate the overflow from the lodge. Several similarly constructed bunkhouses were built behind the lodge just to the south of the Club House. The guest bunkhouse beside the lodge was torn down about 1921, but the bunkhouses behind the lodge continued to serve into the 1940s as quarters for Pahaska employees. Manager Fred Garlow announced that with these added guest facilities Pahaska could accommodate 123 people at a time. At this time in 1913 Garlow also revealed plans for expanding electrical lighting, first installed in the lodge in 1910, to other buildings in Pahaska.[3]

The most famous hunt in Pahaska's history, and one which received nationwide publicity, occurred in the fall of 1913. Col. Cody had hunted out of the lodge in 1912, but the event was given little attention in the newspapers. The hunt of 1913, however, was headline news.

On September 10, Albert I, Prince of Monaco, arrived in New York harbor in his yacht, the Hirondelle. No official salute from the United States was given to Albert I, the first reigning prince ever to visit the country. He had notified the United States State Department earlier that his visit was not an official one, that he was on a pleasure visit and was traveling incognito. After a brief shopping tour in New York City to acquire hunting clothes and a sports outfit, the sixty-four-year-old monarch and his party boarded a train for Cody, Wyoming. His objective, he informed reporters, was to do some shooting and possibly kill a grizzly bear or two. On September 15, the Prince arrived in Cody as the guest of his old friend, A. A. Anderson.[3]

Meanwhile, Col. Cody, who was looking forward to the Prince's visit and a hunting trip to Pahaska, was having serious difficulties. His Wild West show, in combination with Pawnee Bill's Great Far East Show, had gone into bankruptcy in July and the show properties sold at auction in Denver the following month. He lost everything except his favorite horse, Isham, which had been successfully bid on by Col. C. J. Bills of Lincoln, Nebraska, and then returned to Cody.[4]

This shattering denouement to a thirty-year career in the Wild West show must have saddened and discouraged the old scout. But very shortly his prospects were brightened by several offers from vaudeville managers in the United States and London. Cody turned them all down and instead turned his attention to the possibility of making moving pictures.

Ironically, it was his old nemesis, Harry H. Tammen, who had helped to push the Wild West show into bankruptcy, who directed Cody's attention to the film industry by offering him a part in a motion picture. Cody turned this offer aside, but hurried to Denver to talk to Tammen about his own idea for making authentic western historical films.

Cody was familiar with the new entertainment medium since Thomas Edison's company had filmed acts from the Wild West show in 1894 and 1898, and Cody himself had had portions of his show filmed in 1908 and 1910. In 1903 Edwin S. Porter produced "The Great Train Robbery," the first dramatically creative American film. The success of this one-reeler inspired the filming of numerous "westerns" which could be viewed in nickelodeons and variety theaters across America. In his moment of despair in 1913 Col. Cody grasped the significance of the motion picture as a new avenue for his career.

Cody's enthusiasm for making western documentary films apparently convinced Tammen and his partner, Frederick G. Bonfils, of the soundness of the project. They immediately began to make arrangements to produce these films. In short order the approval of the use of Army troops was given by the Secretary of War, Lindley M. Garrison, who was visiting in Denver. Permission was soon obtained from the Secretary of the Interior, Franklin L. Lane, to use the Pine Ridge Reservation and to hire any Sioux Indians who would participate.

The Essanay Film Company of Chicago agreed to produce the films and on September 10, 1913, a contract was signed creating the "Colonel W. F. Cody (Buffalo Bill) Historical Pictures Company." The contract gave Cody a one-third interest in the company, and a one-third interest each to the partnership of Tammen and Bonfils and to the Essanay Company.[5]

Two days later the reinvigorated colonel arrived in Cody with Johnny Baker, John Tate, Carlos Miles and other old comrades from the defunct Wild West show. The presence of Charles E. Kaufman of the Essanay Company on the same train and the arrival, a few days later, of Essanay producer Theodore Wharton was evidence that Cody's plan for making western films would start in the city of Cody.[6]

The colonel had hastened back to Cody in order to be on hand for the opening of the Park County Fair, and to greet the Prince of Monaco, who arrived September 15, the day before the fair opened. Col. Cody and a local reception committee greeted the prince as he stepped out of his train coach at the Burlington depot. The royal party also included Captain Reginert, a member of the palace guard; Captain Bouree, the prince's bodyguard and hunter; the prince's valet, H. Engelhardt; his personal physician, Dr. Loucet; and a Parisian artist,

Louis Tinyre, who would produce a portfolio of paintings depicting various scenes of the ensuing hunting expedition. The royal guests got into waiting automobiles and were escorted by a procession of mounted cowboys, cowgirls, and Indians to the Irma Hotel. There the prince was greeted by A. A. Anderson, his principal host for the visit, and by Mayor W. S. Bennett, who gave a welcoming address. This reception also included Crow Indian Chief Plenty Coups, who was in Cody to participate in the county fair. The chief presented a beautifully decorated peace pipe to the prince. Following the reception Col. Cody hosted a dinner at the Irma Hotel for the distinguished visitors and a dozen of Cody's prominent citizens.

The prince had planned to leave immediately with A. A. Anderson for the latter's Palette Ranch, where the prince would begin the first phase of his hunting expedition in the Cody country. Impressed, perhaps, by the warmth of his greeting, the prince changed his plans and decided to remain in Cody for a few days to participate in the opening of the Park County Fair.[7]

On September 16 the fair opened with a parade of cowboys and cowgirls in colorful western attire and horse-drawn floats depicting Park County industries. Chief Plenty Coups and his band of Crows in native regalia led the mounted riders and the wagons down Sheridan Avenue. The prince viewed the passing parade from the balcony of the Irma Hotel. When it was over the Indians formed a circular line in front of the hotel with Col. Cody and Chief Plenty Coups in the middle. Charles Kaufman filmed the assembled group and the Prince of Monaco on the balcony.

Later that day the prince enjoyed a rodeo and a program of Indian dances. The Essanay cameraman was busy recording these and other fair events on film. Cody photographer Fay Hiscock also filmed some of the most interesting events and took fifty to sixty still photographs.

The prince was especially impressed by the Crow warriors and, in recognition of their contributions to the fair, he presented a rifle from his personal collection to Chief Plenty Coups in a ceremony on Sheridan Avenue. The chief reciprocated by presenting his own gift of elk teeth and a beaded Indian belt to the prince.[8]

On the final day of the fair, September 18, the prince left Cody with his retinue in the company of A. A. Anderson. Their destination was the Palette ranch, where the prince would spend the next nine days hunting, fishing, and horseback riding in the surrounding mountains.[9]

On the day following the prince's departure, Theodore Wharton set his cameras up on Sheridan Street and began the direction of a western drama based on events of early Cody. Signs were placed on several old buildings showing them as they were in 1897. There was the "Cody Trading Company," "Hotel De Trego," and "Salune, Last Chance," located at the corner of Sheridan Avenue and Fourth Street (now Twelfth Street). Col. Cody and other local oldtimers including George T. Beck, Henry Dahlem, Hud Darrah, Mrs. Jake Schwoob, Mr. and Mrs. O. D. Marx, W. T. Barron, F. O. Thompson, Dr. Frances Lane and many others assumed roles in the first western produced in Cody.[10] Col. Cody insisted on realism and authenticity in the films, but an out-of-town visitor, George Hamilton, there for the fair viewed the movie making with a jaundiced eye. The Park County Enterprise carried his statement:

> They are 'faking' typical scenes such as are generally supposed to characterize the 'wild and wooly.' Shooting up the town, saloon brawls, throwing the cowboys into the street, riding the ponies into the 'palaces'. . . When the pictures are shown in the East and Europe the natives of those sections will have a weird idea of Wyoming.[11]

What Hamilton had seen in the making was a nickelodeon western typical of those then showing in towns across America.

On September 27, the Prince of Monaco and A. A. Anderson returned to Cody to join Col. Cody for a big game hunt at Pahaska. The colonel had made arrangements with the renowned big game hunter and guide, Fred J. Richard, to outfit and guide the group. The following day the distinguished hunters drove up the picturesque Cody Road to Pahaska. Essanay cameraman Charles Kaufman traveled with this party and recorded parts of the ensuing hunt on motion pictures.

After arriving at Pahaska on September 28, Col. Cody held an open house for the remainder of the day in order to give members of the Park County Automobile Association and other visitors an opportunity to meet Prince Albert. Newspapers across the country had carried stories of the royal visit to Cody, Wyoming. For days the colonel had been deluged with telegrams from people asking or begging permission to join the hunt. Count Rovigno, an Italian nobleman visiting in Los Angeles, claimed he was a friend of the prince and asked to be included in the hunt. Charles G. "Spend-a-Million" Gates, son of the late wealthy industrialist, John W. "Bet-a-Million" Gates, telegraphed Cody that he was joining the party. With a half dozen of his New York friends, he sped across the United States to Cody, arriving there in his private railroad car on September 25. The colonel denied all the invitations except those issued by the prince.

The impetuous Gates overlooked the fact that he was uninvited and hired Ned Frost, Richard's capable partner in their outfitting business, to equip and guide his hunting party. Gates had had an opportunity to meet the prince in Cody when the latter returned from Anderson's ranch. Nonetheless, Gates and his New York friends journeyed to Pahaska on September 28 to participate in the open house—probably still hoping to accompany the prince's hunting expedition. Col. Cody was amicable but firm—Gates's party headed into the mountains in another direction from the prince's party. Gates may have been disappointed, but his party, led by expert guide Ned Frost, had a highly successful hunt. The gregarious, generous playboy's luck only ran out when he returned to Cody. There, soon after his return on October 28, he died suddenly of a reported attack of apoplexy.

Meanwhile the prince was enjoying the hospitality of Pahaska and preparing to leave on his hunt. At the suggestion of Col. Cody, Fred Richard set up a base camp about thirteen miles north of Pahaska near where Torrent Creek flows into the North Fork. On September 29 the prince and his royal party, Col. Cody, A. A. Anderson, Fred H. Garlow and several members of Cody's defunct Wild West show rode their horses up the North Fork to the camp where Richard's crew had erected two large dining tents, a cook tent, and six sleeping tents near the edge of Torrent Creek. Also accompanying this group was United States Ranger Harry E. Miller, assigned as camp guard to the royal party by R. W. Allen, Supervisor of the Shoshone National Forest. Miller unofficially became the camp photographer by recording many scenes of the hunting expedition on his Kodak camera. Merril Synder, another member of the forest service, came along as fire guard, and "Mose" Linderfeldt as cook rounded out the party.

Col. Cody did not hunt, as was usually the case on such parties, but played the host, seeing that his distinguished guest was entertained and comfortable. Former Wild West associates Carlos Miles, an expert rope spinner, and John Tate, a yarn spinner, were there to provide diversions.

The prince enjoyed the entertainment and conversations around the nightly campfires, but he had no taste for lying around camp. He had been frustrated on his earlier hunt with Anderson at only shooting geese, ducks, grouse, and sage hens. Albert was an

Campfire scene at Camp Monaco, 1913. From the left seated on chairs are Abraham Archibald Anderson, designer of Pahaska Lodge; Albert I, Prince of Monaco; and Col. Cody. Seated on the ground from the left are Dr. Loucet, the prince's physician; Parisian artist Louis Tinyre; and an unidentified member of the royal party. From the Buffalo Bill album.
Photo courtesy Peg Garlow, Cody, Wyoming.

experienced hunter—he wanted big game. On September 30, the day after the party had arrived at camp, the prince was ready to hunt. Captain Bouree, the prince's bodyguard and hunter, had expected to be at his master's side at all times. Fred Richard, however, insisted that while two could easily hunt together, a party of three would make too much noise. The prince agreed, and with the essentials for a side camp—bedding, food and cooking utensils—he and Fred Richard rode into the rugged Absarokas.

A herd of elk were sighted the following day, and the prince shot a large bull elk. The prince stayed beside his fallen trophy while Richard rode back to camp for assistance in bringing the meat out. Later, Captain Bouree, who was trained in taxidermy, brought the elk's hide, horns and bones back to the main camp, and artist Louis Tinyre painted the scene where the elk had been shot, to provide the proper background for the mounted elk in the Monaco museum.

Even as Col. Cody was preparing for this hunt with the prince, Indians and army troops and Essanay cameramen were gathering at Pine Ridge Agency in South Dakota preparatory to filming of historical documentaries. Cody had an obligation to be there as a principal actor, and he was eager to get started with what appeared to be a promising new career in film making. His new project was never to be a financial success, but at this moment the colonel had high hopes. Regretting to leave the prince, but under pressure of time, Cody rode out of camp on October 2 only four days after arriving in the mountains. Fred Garlow, John Tate and Essanay cameraman Charles E. Kaufman accompanied the colonel back to Cody where the latter and Kaufman soon entrained for the Pine Ridge Agency.

A. A. Anderson assumed Cody's mantle as host, and the prince continued his quest for big game. With an elk secured, the prince then wanted a bear. Richard realized that their chances were slim, since the spring season with its more abundant food supply was a better time for hunting bear. To improve their opportunities for finding one, Richard moved the camp a few miles downstream where abundant ripe berries might attract Mr. Bruin. Before leaving the camp, which the prince had found an idyllic place, Ranger Harry E. Miller carved a flat place on a spruce tree and Louis Tinyre painted the words "Camp Monaco 1913." The tree stands there today as a reminder of the famous hunt, the inscription now somewhat obscured by the healing growth around it.

Snow had begun to fall as the second camp was set up, and the hunters took advantage of it to follow the tracks of a bear which was working its way down the mountainside to a berry patch along a stream. A fairly large black bear was finally sighted, and soon the prince's powerful rifle claimed another trophy. The taxidermist and artist again appeared to do their work. The prince regarded Fred Richard as a master guide and hunter and made plans with him for a big game hunt in the Kodiak Islands and Alaska the following year. He was to meet Richard in Seattle, and they would proceed northward to the hunting areas aboard the royal yacht. The onset of World War I intervened, however, and the proposed trip never became a reality.

On October 13, the royal hunting party broke camp and left the Pahaska-North Fork country for Cody. There the hides and bones of the elk and bear were turned over to Cody taxidermist George Richard, who prepared them for shipment to Monaco. On October 15 the prince left Cody in a special car provided by the Burlington Railroad. En route to Chicago he was interviewed by a reporter and left these impressions of his Wyoming visit: "I rode a horse, and

I like the personalities in the West. Men are real out there. I like Colonel Cody more than I can say." Later, at a farewell dinner held for him in New York City, he commented on the success of his Wyoming hunt and warmly praised the western hospitality he had enjoyed.[12]

Before Pahaska opened its doors for business in 1914, two deaths occurred there under rather unusual circumstances. In March John Robert Davies, better known locally as John "Reckless," accompanied by Milt Benedict and Bert Oliver, had left for Pahaska to put up ice. Davies had been the intimate friend and hunting companion of Col. Cody for many years, and at this time was employed as a handyman by the colonel.

A cavernous one-and-a-half story log ice house had been erected a hundred yards or more to the right of the lodge. During the winter, ice was cut from the frozen North Fork River in large blocks and stacked in the ice house. Thick insulating layers of sawdust separated and covered the blocks. In the days before electrical refrigeration, this was the standard means of ensuring an ice supply for the preservation of perishables throughout the summer.

The ice crew was heavily dependent upon canned goods for food, and, unfortunately, one day they consumed a tainted can of green beans. John Reckless didn't like their taste and ate only a few of the beans, while his companions ate the rest. They became violently ill and disgorged the beans, while John retained his and became steadily sicker. He was brought to Cody and died suddenly in his room at the Irma Hotel from what was reported as ptomaine poisoning.[13]

The newspaper which announced Davies' death on March 25, 1914, also carried a long account of the mysterious death of the twenty-six-year-old Edna Durell, who had been found dead several days earlier on the road between Pahaska and the soldier's station at the east entrance to Yellowstone National Park. Miss Durell had been employed as a waitress at Pahaska the previous summer. When her employment terminated at the end of the tourist season, she had rented one of Pahaska's guest cabins and spent the winter setting out and caring for trap lines. The hardy lady was also having a romantic affair with Sergeant James Brooks, who was in charge of the soldier's station located two miles away at the east entrance. The mystery surrounding her death centered upon her reasons for setting out through the snow for the soldier's station in the late afternoon or evening in four degrees above zero temperatures wearing only a short-sleeved house dress and no coat or hat. Her tracks indicated that she had walked to within three hundred yards of the station and then unaccountably had turned around and headed back down the road. Her frozen body was found the following morning by Sergeant Brooks, who then telephoned Deputy Sheriff E. S. Hoopes of Cody. The sheriff and a small party came from Cody by automobile to Holm Lodge, where deep snow forced them to continue by horse-drawn wagons to Pahaska. From there, with the assistance of Mr. and Mrs. George Walliker, the resident managers at Pahaska, they brought the body back to the lodge on a hand sled. The body was placed in one of the unheated lodge rooms that opened out to the left side porch. In the morning the body was taken to Cody for a medical examination. The inquest that was held to consider the causes of Miss Durell's strange behavior considered the possibilities of suicide and poisoning, but concluded that neither of these was logical. The circumstances behind Miss Durell's death remain a mystery.[14]

About three months after these unfortunate deaths Pahaska was opened for summer guests. Paul C. Blum, one of Col. Cody's early associates in the Wild West show, had been appointed general manager of the Irma and Pahaska to replace Fred Garlow. In the fall of 1913, Garlow had been called to South Dakota by Col. Cody to assist him in the production and marketing of films that were being produced at the Pine Ridge Indian Reservation. Blum announced that Pahaska had been renovated, remodeled, and enlarged and would receive guests on June 1.

Among the new additions to Pahaska's tourist facilities in 1914 was a new garage. After 1910, increasing numbers of visitors were driving their own automobiles to Pahaska. Pahaska's managers, quite naturally, were eager to please and in every way encourage the auto traveler. The carriage house, built in 1905 in the era of horse and buggy, was clearly inadequate in the age of the automobile. Hence, early in 1913, a large two-story log garage with a shed-type roof was constructed just to the west of the carriage house and about one hundred feet to the rear right side of the lodge. After several years' service as a garage, this shed-roof structure was converted to other uses. The north end was used as a carpentry shop, with the rest of the first floor remodeled into an apartment for Pahaska's workers. The upstairs was used as a general storage area and resulted in the building being called the Mystery House. It was a "mystery" how anyone could find anything in the hodgepodge of storage items.[15]

Manager Blum apparently felt that more garage accommodations were needed, because in 1914 he announced the construction of yet another garage at Pahaska. This one was to be located several

Mystery House at Pahaska. Originally constructed in 1913 as a garage, this large log structure was eventually divided up for use as a carpentry shop, employee apartments and general storage. Photo courtesy Jessie B. Kensel, Ellensburg, Washington.

hundred feet to the west of the lodge along the north side of the Cody Road. A bunkhouse extension for employees was built onto the east side of the garage. Quite possibly this garage-bunkhouse structure was erected with some of the lumber salvaged from the Wapiti Inn, since its vertical board wall construction was similar to that of the Inn.

In the following year Fred H. Garlow again assumed the management of Pahaska. He had the garage along the Cody Road torn down, but left the attached bunkhouse standing as a separate building. Garlow then had constructed, in the same location, a large log garage which offered Pahaska's first auto repair and fuel service. Earlier garages had merely provided sheltered parking.

Cody Boal, the colonel's grandson, was the resident manager at Pahaska during the 1914 tourist season. The lodge again enjoyed a busy season as it had since 1911, when auto-transported guests began coming up the Cody Road in greater numbers. The Wylie Transportation Company continued its practice, begun two years earlier, of transporting its guests directly to Pahaska, where they were given meals and lodging.[16]

Pahaska

Buffalo Bill's Ideal Summer
Resort in the Mountains......

Open June 1

Enlarged, Improved, and
Better than ever.

New Garage

PARTICULARS AT

The Irma Hotel

Cody, Wyoming

Figure 10: This advertisement appeared in the Park County Enterprise *throughout the summer of 1914.*

No special events were advertised for the 1914 season at Pahaska, but in August the Park County Automobile Association followed its customary practice of holding its annual meeting at the Club House, followed by a dinner and dance.

Cody Boal left for school at North Platte, Nebraska, at the end of August, and Mr. and Mrs. W. D. Knott moved in as winter caretakers. The closure of the 1914 season was marred by Paul Blum's death in December. By the end of the month, Fred Garlow had again been appointed manager of the Irma Hotel and Pahaska.[17]

6 Autos to Yellowstone National Park

The biggest news of 1915 came on April 21, when Secretary of the Interior Franklin K. Lane authorized the admission of pleasure vehicles into Yellowstone National Park beginning on August 1. For the past several years, in anticipation of this event, road crews had been busy grading and widening the entrance roads to the park and the belt line roads within it. Construction was begun in 1915 on three new steel bridges over the North Fork River, including one a few hundred feet below Pahaska. These new bridges were completed by 1917, replacing the old log bridges, which were too narrow and too decrepit to accommodate the increasing volume of automobile traffic.[1]

News of the coming admission of automobiles into the park spurred the Cody Club to action. At its meeting in April 1915, Dave Jones suggested that a "canyon bee" should be sponsored by the Cody Club for the purpose of improving the canyon road. The idea of the canyon bee was to get volunteers to donate one day's work on the road. The Cody Club members approved Jones's suggestion unanimously and appointed a committee composed of Jones, George T. Beck and Howard F. Bell to make the arrangements. June 24th was set as "Canyon Bee Day" and the *Park County Enterprise* gave the coming event front page coverage. Thirty Cody men appeared for work on June 24th, most of them merchants and professional people. The Cody Club furnished them with donated picks and shovels and work began at the entrance of Shoshone Canyon. D. E. Hollister furnished a team of horses, and Cody businessmen who could not work themselves for one reason or another provided funds to keep the team and four men working on the road for 100 days. Canyon Bee Day was judged an "entire success" by the newspaper, which noted that rocks and debris were removed from a long stretch of road and that twenty-five loads of dirt were dumped to improve the grade at the canyon entrance.[2]

Canyon Bee Day in 1915 was a logical response of Codyites who understood that anything done to improve the road to the park would make the East Entrance more attractive to tourists and hence would mean more publicity and business for their city. The larger profits derived from increased tourism were not limited to Cody. Every dude ranch and resort along the Cody Road, including Pahaska, would benefit from improved roads. Volunteer work on the road was good for business and the practice continued. In July 1918, for instance, the *Park County Enterprise* announced a "good roads" day. Volunteers were asked to bring picks, shovels and rakes and be prepared to spend a full day clearing rock out of the road through the canyon.[3]

The canyon road and Sylvan Pass were the two major problem areas of the Cody Road. Aside from the extreme grades and narrow roadway, the biggest problem at Sylvan Pass was clearing the road of snow in June or July so that tourists could get through to the park. S. P. Van Arsdall of Cody recalls that in June 1920 he accompanied a crew of twenty-four men who had volunteered to shovel snow at Sylvan Pass. A camp was set up about three miles inside the East Entrance and the men went to work. Ranger Tex Wisdom and a park engineer used T.N.T. to blast out the deeper drifts, but where the snow lay only two to three feet deep it was shoveled out to the width of a single car lane. The newspaper report of this activity noted that the shoveling had begun on Friday and by Saturday the men had cleared the road of snow nearly to the top of the pass.[4]

In addition to routine road repair and snow shoveling, Cody volunteers also responded to emergency situations. In 1918 flood waters resulting from the sudden melting of snow in the late spring caused a great deal of damage to the Cody Road. The park service repaired that part of the road within the borders of the park. In his annual report for 1918, the Director of the National Park Service noted:

> As for that part of the road lying outside of park boundaries, repairs were wholly the work of public-spirited citizens of Cody. These men closed the doors of the business houses and, taking tools and supplies in their automobiles, proceeded far up into the mountains and accomplished the enormous labor necessary to make the park accessible to motorists using the entrance highway. The personal sacrifices were great, and I want to express here publicly to the Cody people, as I have already expressed it personally, our deep appreciation of their efforts.[5]

On Sunday, July 22, 1923, Horace M. Albright, Superintendent of Yellowstone National Park, telephoned Dave Jones in Cody to report that a tremendous cloudburst had washed out bridges and severely damaged the Cody Road. Jones and Kid Wilson immediately sent a truckload of bridge timbers and a crew of twenty men up the North Fork. According to the *Cody Enterprise*,

> The citizens of Cody, responding nobly to the call for volunteers, dropped their business affairs and rushed to the scene, taking with them all the picks and shovels that the town and forest service could supply, with the result that by eight o'clock Monday night, cars from Pahaska had safely made the trip to Cody.
> The men who assumed active charge of the work are loud in their praise of the way in which the volunteer workers plunged into the task of clearing the road, as they often worked in mud and water knee-deep.[6]

Keeping the road open to the park was important to Cody people for business reasons, but the extent of their sacrifices in volunteer work clearly demonstrates a selfless public-spirited attitude that went beyond purely business motivations.

Pahaska manager Fred H. Garlow responded to the beginning of the auto age in Yellowstone National Park in 1915 by announcing the construction of a new log garage that would carry a full line of supplies for automobiles, including gasoline and oil. The small frame garage that manager Paul Blum had built in 1914 was apparently considered inadequate for the needs of increasing auto traffic and was torn down. The adjoining bunkhouse was left to stand as a separate building and continued to house Pahaska garagemen until 1929, when it too was removed. A large log garage was constructed in June 1915, on the same site as Blum's garage, on the north side of the Cody Road, west of the lodge, a hundred feet or more beyond the last guest cabin. Gus Holm, who operated Holm's Auto Repair Company in Cody, was granted a concession by Garlow to operate the new Pahaska Garage. This structure remained in use for nearly fifty years, when it was replaced by a small service station. At that time, the log garage was moved several hundred feet north of its original location where it serves today as a utility building.[7]

Meanwhile the transportation companies with offices in Cody were making preparations for the 1915 tourist season. The Holm Company announced in May that it had already booked large parties of tourists and that four White Steamers were standing by to transport them to the park. The Wylie Company, which had previously contracted with the Holm Company to carry Wylie guests to Pahaska, transferred its carrying business to Edgar D. "Kid" Wilson and Joe Wolf. Wilson and Wolf had purchased a new White gas car to carry the Wylie tourists at Pahaska. After the tourists had been fed and lodged overnight they were taken to the east entrance, where Wylie's horse-drawn wagons and coaches picked them up for transportation through the park.[8]

Early in July 1915, the Appropriation Committee of the United States Congress arrived in Cody for a pre-opening examination of the Cody Road to the park. A procession of cars led by Jake Schwoob carried the committee members up the road to Pahaska. The party had lunch at the lodge, but then drove up Sylvan Pass to the Lake Hotel without difficulties. The committee gave unstinted praise to the Cody Road and the way was paved for the grand opening on August 1. Jake Schwoob and his passengers in the lead car, including Committee Chairman J. Fitzgerald and Congressman F. W. Mondell, enjoyed the honor of being in the first automobiles to enter Yellowstone National Park by the east entrance.[9]

Mrs. Fred Garlow, the resident manager of Pahaska in 1915, announced that a reception and dance would be held at the lodge on the evening of July 31 to celebrate the official opening of the park to automobiles the following day. On July 28 the Entrance Day Committee in Cody exulted in the fact that there were about twenty cars in Cody waiting for the big day. One car was from Massachusetts, two from Florida, several from Colorado, and a number of others from the southwestern states. Other cars had already gone up the North Fork to wait at Holm Lodge or Pahaska. Heavy rains in the Cody area and throughout the West just prior to the opening made the entrance roads slippery and dangerous. Despite this, Pahaska and Holm Lodge were booked full of tourists on July 30th and 31st and the public reception at Pahaska was heavily attended. On August 1, sixteen cars passed through the east entrance and by the end of the park season 193 were recorded. In total, some 958 cars had entered from all four entrances. In September Mrs. Garlow reported that Pahaska had experienced the biggest season in its history (see fig. 11 for Pahaska's rates).[10]

In 1916 the Holm Transportation Company went bankrupt. The company had prospered for a time, but the opening of Yellowstone National Park in 1915 to private automobiles, and increasing competition from other transportation companies severely diminished the number of tourists carried into the park by the Holm group. This

Pahaska Tepee Rates, 1915

Hotel and Tent Rooms, per day .... $ 3.00
Hotel and Ten Rooms, per week $18.00
Saddle Horses, per day .... $ 1.50
Furnished Single Cabin per week $15.00
   (Light and wood furnished)
Furnished Double Cabin per week $20.00
Baths .... .50
Auto fare from Cody, each way .... $ 5.00
A rate of $100.00 per month includes saddle horse

Figure 11: From the Park County Enterprise, *July 21, 1915.*

bankruptcy prompted the formation of the Cody-Sylvan Pass Motor Company in 1916 for the purpose of transporting tourists from Cody to Yellowstone National Park. The new company was created by a merger of the Yellowstone National Park Transportation Company, the Yellowstone-Western Stage Company, the Wylie Permanent Camping Company, and the Shaw and Powell Camping Company, which had been operating transportation and camping facilities under permit in the park for a number of years. It was obviously important to their combined interests to maintain the flow of tourists from the Burlington station in Cody to the park. The failure of the Holm enterprise undoubtedly suggested that substantial capitalization and a monopoly of the transportation business were essential to success— and the combination of these various interests were designed to provide these ingredients. A. W. Miles, general manager of the Wylie Company, was responsible for the formation of the new company, and Frank Jay Haynes, who had an interest in the Wylie Company, played a role in its management. The Cody-Sylvan Pass Motor Company used the defunct Holm Company's barn and equipment in Cody, but there is no record that Tex Holm was in any way personally connected with the new company.[11]

On July 6, 1916, the Department of the Interior authorized the Cody-Sylvan Pass Motor Company to establish an automobile transportation line to accommodate tourists wishing to enter the park by the east entrance. The company purchased seven eleven-passenger White touring cars and eight seven-passenger M55 Buicks. Wire-enclosed General Motors trucks were used for hauling baggage. Kid Wilson was appointed the local manager of the new company. The reminiscences of Kid Wilson provide an interesting account of the operations of the Cody-Sylvan Pass Motor Company.

> We left Cody about eight in the morning, making the fifty-three miles to Pahaska for lunch. We were supposed to cover the thirty-four miles to Lake Junction by 4:30 P.M., giving us an average of ten miles per hour. We passed or met plenty of 'sage brushers,' wagons and teams. They had the right of way and always pulled to the inside of the road and stopped. The drivers would get out and hold the horses, who weren't about to stand still and let a car pass within a foot or so of them. Sometimes it was necessary to unhitch the horses and lead them off the road before we could drive past.
>
> It was upgrade from Cody to the top of Sylvan Pass, and up and down from there to Lake Junction. An average of fifteen miles an hour was good, and could only be made if the road was dry. Climbing from Pahaska to the top of the pass, the road followed a gulch with double 'S' switchbacks and a circular bridge. If we were late getting to the Lake Hotel, we had to wait until the horse-drawn coaches were unloaded and away before we were allowed to arrive.[12]

In 1916, the Cody-Sylvan Pass Motor Company carried a total of 1,293 passengers into the park as far as the Lake Hotel. The outbound passengers were also given lunch at Pahaska.

David M. Steele, Rector of the Church of St. Luke in Philadelphia, was a passenger on a Cody-Sylvan Pass auto in 1916. His impressions of his journey into Yellowstone National Park from Cody were recorded in his book *Going Abroad Overland*. Steele's unrestrained sarcasm and eloquence have left us a memorable picture of one man's impressions of the town of Cody and of an automobile trip up the Cody Road to the park:

> The distance between these [Cody and Yellowstone National Park] is one day's journey of eighty-six miles, which can now be made upon smooth-rolling ten-passenger new auto busses (sic).
>
> The family name of Cody will not exactly be immortalized by the town's hostelry, the Hotel Irma; but let that pass—like the sleepless night it gave us. There is soon a better to be builded. This is a woeful example of how incompetent the management can be of a monopoly. There is nepotism in appointment, absentee ownership, indifferent attention, lack of all efficiency, and Western ignorance of Eastern requirement of what it takes to make a tourist even moderately comfortable. In fact, the whole town seems to be here only because it came along one day and, startled into awe by the surrounding scenery, stopped short and has stayed ever since. The scene about the city at close hand is one of isolation, not to say of desolation. Concrete pavements run with the same regularity as chalk marks on a tennis court. They lie as white and blazing in the sun and over earth as bare and solid, as dry and as unproductive.
>
> But we left early this bleak, sun-baked, almost sheepless sheep country, and passed westward from the city, with its 1,500 stranded population and its sulphur mills adjoining it as torches in a picture of Inferno. Five miles out, on glancing back, we were not only glad that we had left it, but that we had this far sight of it.[13]

As Frank O. Thompson, driver and tour guide, steered his Cody-Sylvan Pass auto westward, Steele recorded a constant flow of impressions about the canyon, Shoshone Dam, the Holy City, and other scenic beauties of the Cody Road. Codyites who might have welcomed the opportunity to tar and feather Steele for his uncomplimentary remarks about their town would have cheered him for his laudatory descriptions of the Cody Road:

> This Cody Road has almost all the features of all the famous sight-seeing places combined in this country. It has features severally grander than their greatest ones in series. The Shoshone Canyon, through the bottom of which we rode, is as deep as the Yellowstone Canyon, from the brink of

which later we looked down. The snow-capped mountains all about us, although at a distance, were impressive as the Selkirk Range on the Canadian Pacific. The falls of the Yellowstone are as fine as Niagara. Frost's Caves, under Cedar Mountain, are as extensive as those in Kentucky. The approach to the Absaroka Range is between rock walls as narrow, looking up to peaks as precipitous, as in and through the Royal Gorge on the Denver and Rio Grande. . .

I had never enjoyed a single day's journey so much in my life. And such was the composite verdict of our complex company. If enthusiasm waned at any point, it was only because of multiplicity of wonders, for we rode entranced until new marvels by the mile grew commonplace. The sustained beauty and grandeur of this scenery is greater than within the Park itself. And yet this road is so new people scarcely know it exists. The truth about it writes like fiction and the simplest facts read like romance. This Cody Road is a fitting monument to the memory of him whose name it bears, to Colonel Cody.[14]

Steele mentioned stopping at Pahaska for lunch but failed to record what might have been the most vivid description ever made of the lodge. Other tourists like Steele came up the Cody Road in droves in 1916. The annual reports of the Superintendent of Yellowstone National Park show that 4,593 people entered the park through the east entrance compared to 1,550 in 1915. In 1917 the number would jump to 6,935. Although there are no existing business records for this period, Pahaska must have enjoyed increasing revenues. As the tourist traffic increased, dude ranches began to crop up in the Cody area. In 1915, I. H. Larom and W. H. Brooks of New York purchased James McLaughlin's Valley Ranch on the South Fork. Under the astute management of Larom, Valley Ranch would develop into one of the finest dude ranches in the West. Blackwater Camp, also opened in 1915, was located on the North Fork about thirteen miles east of Pahaska. B. C. Rumsey and George T. Beck started Blackwater Camp as a summer camp for boys. Later Rumsey bought out Beck's interests and established a dude ranch there.[15]

The Cody-Sylvan Pass Motor Company was in existence for one brief year, and then was closed down as a result of an extensive reorganization of the concession system in Yellowstone National Park in 1917. Various corporations and individuals had for years furnished transportation services, camp and hotel accommodations, and photographic services to visiting tourists in the park. This hodge-podge of interests led to duplication of services and facilities. The end result of this was often inefficient and uneconomical service for the traveling public. In addition, the use of automobiles on the same roads with horse-drawn coaches had caused great difficulties. The logical solution appeared to be the motorization of all transportation in the park. Early in 1917 the Director of the National Park Service approved the merger of all hotel and transportation companies in the park under the management of Harry W. Child. Child, who already had a controlling interest in the Yellowstone Park Hotel and the Yellowstone National Park Transportation Company, was allowed to buy out the Yellowstone-Western Stage Company, the Wylie Permanent Camping Company, and the Shaw and Powell Camping Company. Thus the various interests which had created the Cody-Sylvan Pass Motor Company were consolidated under Child's management. This company, then, obtained complete control of the public transportation of tourists into and throughout the park. Child purchased 110 passenger buses and sixteen seven-passenger cars—the horse and stagecoach era of Yellowstone National Park passed into history. The yellow buses of the Yellowstone Park Transportation Company soon became familiar sights on the Cody Road.[16]

These reforms in transportation and lodging services were designed to make Yellowstone National Park a more attractive destination for tourists. These improvements and the increasing use of private automobiles for vacation travel augured well for the business prospects of the Irma Hotel and Pahaska. The changes, however, came too late to be of much benefit to Col. Cody. By 1916 his health was failing badly, his mining interests were unrewarding, and his career as a western showman was in precipitous decline. Ironically, Cody's last recorded visit to Pahaska in the spring of 1915 was to show the place to Col. P. J. Durbin of Los Angeles, who expressed some interest in buying it. Durbin, headlined in a Cody newspaper as the biggest hog raiser in the West, was apparently interested in buying the Irma Hotel as well. The financially beleaguered Cody was willing to sell, but Durbin soon dropped any plans to invest in the Cody enterprises. By the end of 1915, Col. Cody was reduced to converting his beloved TE Ranch into a dude ranch to help raise badly needed funds. He died in Denver on January 10, 1917.[17]

Meanwhile, Fred Garlow, manager of the Irma, was making

arrangements for extensive improvements to the hotel. Large numbers of tourists were expected during the summer of 1917, and Garlow stated that he wished to provide the finest hotel services possible. The anticipated profits apparently did not materialize, or possibly there were unusual expenses to be met in the settlement of Col. Cody's estate. In any case, an advertisement appeared in the newspaper in August offering both the Irma Hotel and Pahaska Tepee for sale (fig. 12). The Sweeney Ranch, also owned by Mrs. Louisa Cody, the colonel's widow, was advertised for sale in July. The Irma Hotel was not sold until 1921, after Mrs. Cody's death. Pahaska, however, was sold in October, 1917, to Mrs. Edwin "Lulu" Hall, a widow from Roundup, Montana, for an estimated $12,000.[18]

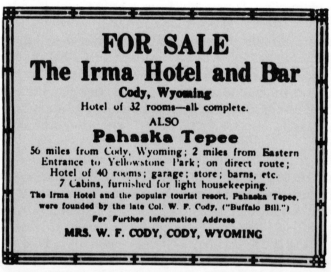

Figure 12: This advertisement ran in consecutive issues in 1917 in the Park County Enterprise; *August 15, 22, 29; September 5, 12, 19, 26; and October 3, 10.*

7 New Owners - Montanans Lulu Hall And Jack F. Files

America's involvement in World War I and a false rumor that Yellowstone National Park had been closed for the summer of 1918 (only the hotels had been closed), reduced the number of tourists entering through the east entrance that year to 4,467, down from 6,935 in 1917. Pahaska's tourist business fell off correspondingly, although local news columns continued to comment on the popularity of the place with local people, who would spend a week or more vacationing there. Newspaper advertising of Pahaska's services, which had been fairly regular from 1906 to 1917, was reduced to only occasional ads after this time. Lulu Hall, the new owner of Pahaska, did not advertise the lodge at all and subsequent owners did very little. Perhaps the increasing volume of tourists coming up the Cody Road after 1918 made extensive advertising unnecessary.[1]

The number of tourists entering the park through the east entrance increased dramatically from 4,467 in 1918 to 13,455 in 1919. Francis T. Hayden of Cody was employed as a bus driver for the Yellowstone Park Transportation Company for several years beginning in 1918. He recalls that he picked up tourists at the Burlington train station in Cody and transported them either to Canyon Hotel or the Lake Hotel in Yellowstone National Park. The driver stayed overnight in the park and then returned with a busload of tourists to Cody the next day. According to Hayden, the buses stopped at Pahaska for lunch on both legs of the journey. The meal was included as a part of the cost of the tour ticket. Hayden remembers that he and the tourists sat down to a lunch served family style at tables in the long dining room behind the lodge fireplace.[2]

A. R. "Brownie" Newton of Cody went to work for Lulu Hall at Pahaska soon after his return from World War I service in Europe. Employed as a handyman, he worked wherever he was needed, including being the cook at times. One of his fellow workers in 1919 was Billy Monday, who later gained local fame as Cody's pioneer aviator. Monday at this time was Mrs. Hall's chauffeur and drove her

Mrs. Edwin C. "Lulu" Hall, owner of Pahaska, 1917-1924.
Photo courtesy Edwin L. Hall, Columbia Falls, Montana.

Cadillac to Cody as needed to bring supplies to the lodge. Kid Wilson operated an auto taxi service between Cody and the East Entrance. His wife, Sybil, was a familiar figure at the lodge, bringing tourists up the Cody Road to Pahaska or to dude ranches along the way.[3]

Lulu Hall initiated few changes or improvements at Pahaska during her period of management. The newspaper did note that in 1919 mechanics of the Forsyth (Montana) Motor and Electric Company installed a new Matthews diesel electric lighting system at a cost of several thousand dollars. This is apparently the only significant investment she made at Pahaska. Mrs. Hall, heavyset and in her fifties, seemed to enjoy the social life of Cody more than the relative isolation of Pahaska. During the winter she hosted a number of dinners for friends in her rooms at the Irma Hotel. By 1919 she was clearly a social leader in Cody, with her various activities being regularly reported in the local newspaper columns. In March 1920, for instance, she sponsored a dance for the benefit of Fred Coe Post No. 20, American Legion. The dance was held on April 20 and brought in over $100.00. She was complimented in the paper for her generous support of the Legion, and in future years she continued her sponsorship of this annual benefit dance. It was perhaps this preference for town life that prompted Lulu Hall to lease Pahaska to Jack F. Files of Forsyth, Montana, in the spring of 1920.[4]

Mrs. Hall's lawyer, F. V. H. Collins of Forsyth, was also the friend and lawyer of Jack Files. Files apparently had learned through Collins that Mrs. Hall was interested in leasing Pahaska. Files had already had twenty years of experience in the restaurant business in Forsyth when he signed the lease, and he proved to be an able and energetic manager of Pahaska. Travel through the east entrance to Yellowstone National Park increased rapidly throughout the 1920s. During the four years that Files operated Pahaska travel through the east entrance jumped from 19,868 tourists in 1920 to 39,687 in 1924. These figures are reflected in a newspaper report in August 1920, which stated that 400 people had been served dinner at Pahaska in the record period of two hours and fifteen minutes. After the highly successful season of 1920, Files ecstatically reported to the newspaper:

> Our success up here has been unprecedented and unlooked for. It has been so great and promises so well for the future that I contemplate building on a dining room next season large enough to accommodate 250 persons. We intend to make other improvements also for the outlook justifies the expense even in these days of higher cost of labor and building material.[5]

Two months later Lloyd Evans left for Pahaska to help in the building of a large dining room, thirty by eighty-four feet, with fourteen sleeping apartments above. Construction of the new dining room commenced in earnest the following March (1921), with twelve carpenters busy at work on the two-story structure. The new building was attached directly to the rear of the lodge and opened into the

*Jack F. and Emma Files, Managers of Pahaska for Lulu Hall,
1920-1924; and owners of Pahaska, January - May 1924.*
Photo courtesy Alice F. Donnell, Worland, Wyoming.

lodge on two levels. Upon entering the lodge one could walk directly through it, passing the stone fireplace by entrances on either side, and proceeding across the old dining room to the entrance of the new. A large round wood stove had been set up towards the end of the dining room to furnish heat, and just beyond that was the new kitchen with its large wood range. The upper level, above the dining room, contained new guest rooms and opened directly into the mezzanine gallery of the lodge. The new rooms were reached by using the stairway on the left side of the lobby. For the first time in its history, Pahaska had modern plumbing when Files added one upstairs bathroom for men and another for women.[6]

On June 18, 1921, the formal opening of Pahaska was held with a supper and a dance. Files had continued the contract begun by Mrs. Hall to serve tourists traveling to and from the park in the yellow buses of the Yellowstone Park Transportation Company. The new structure built onto the lodge greatly expanded dining facilities, and several hundred guests were served regularly every day through the summer. The bus tourists did not stay overnight, but vacationers might stay a week or more, and the increasing number of Yellowstone-bound tourists driving their own autos used Pahaska's enlarged lodging facilities. Holm Lodge, Blackwater Camp, the Fred Morris Ranch, the P Bar P Ranch of Lawrence and Pete Nordquist were all located near the Cody Road. These dude ranches furnished little competition to Pahaska, because they were catering to guests who contracted to stay for long terms rather than transients. Pahaska would at times have long-term guests and would conduct quasi-dude ranch functions in furnishing guides and horses and in outfitting hunting trips. For the most part, Pahaska was a mountain resort—its primary income derived from serving the needs of the passing tourists.

Files did not use the small log cabin to the rear left of the lodge for a store, as had been customary. Instead, he set up a small grocery section in the lodge where tourists and campers would buy drugs, books, toilet articles, bread, canned goods, and other supplies. A showcase in the lodge displayed high quality curio items—Indian jewelry, Alaska walrus ivory beads, Navaho rugs, Chimayo blankets, baskets, and other kinds of Indian goods.

About sixty people worked at Pahaska under the direction of Jack Files. These included waitresses, kitchen help, wood choppers, horse wranglers and handymen. Mrs. George (Alice) Donnell, daughter of Files, stated that she kept books and worked in the store, and that her mother, Emma, and her sisters also worked at Pahaska.[7]

Pahaska did not own horses, but Tex Kennedy, a popular young wrangler in the Cody country, operated a horse concession there for several years. He kept eight to ten horses in the corrals at Pahaska and took dudes on horseback trips in the surrounding mountains. In the fall he acted as a guide for hunting parties. Kennedy arrived in the Cody country in 1914 and was manager of the Fred Morris dude ranch for five years before taking charge of the horses at Pahaska.

Kennedy was adept at leather work and specialized in making high quality men's and women's jackets. During the winter of 1923-24, he joined Ed Bohlin, a former Cody saddle maker in Hollywood, California, where Bohlin operated the Novelty Leather Shop. Bohlin had contracts from several motion picture companies to make fancy saddles and leather trappings for use in western films. Kennedy assisted Bohlin in this work during the winter, and then returned to Pahaska in the late spring of 1924 to operate his horse concession. Kennedy's fine quality leather shirts and jackets continued in future years to be in great demand in the Big Horn Basin. Later, after leaving Pahaska, the versatile Kennedy became a deputy game warden in Park County.[8]

Kennedy's partner in the horse concession at Pahaska from 1921 to 1923 was Alexis F. Chapaton. Chapaton, a young man of means, had come to the Cody country from Los Angeles about 1918, and had become acquainted with Tex Kennedy. Chapaton had originally come to Wyoming for his health, but he became entranced with the western life and particularly with life in the upper North Fork Valley. Chapaton liked Pahaska so well that he obtained a permit from the United States Forest Service and, with the help of Kennedy and others, built an attractive log cabin across the North Fork from Pahaska in 1922. Chapaton unfortunately did not have long to enjoy his western idyll. He died in a hospital in Detroit, Michigan, on December 5, 1923, following a serious operation. The Chapaton Cabin was acquired later by Pahaska owners, and was rented out during the summer. This well-known cabin, which lay beside the present Pahaska-Sunlight Trail, was torn down a number of years ago.[9]

In 1922, for the first time, more automobiles were driven into Yellowstone National Park through the east entrance than through any other gate. In 1923, the east entrance fell into second place, but regained first place in 1924 and held this position through 1928. The growing popularity of the Cody Road for auto tourists opened glowing prospects for profits to those businesses catering to the tourist trade. Jack Files was among those who grasped this opportunity. In January 1922, Files expanded his business activities in the Cody country by assuming management of the Irma Hotel. When Grover Wray's lease to operate the Irma dining room expired on March 1, 1924, Files then accepted this responsibility as well. Data compiled by *The Cody Enterprise* in mid-July 1923 indicated that Pahaska had served meals to 7,602 tourists since the season had opened and that the lodge's room accommodations had been filled every day. In Cody, the Irma, the Chamberlain, the Ainsworth Inn, and other hotels and boarding houses were full, and the Cody campground for auto tourists averaged 100 automobiles a night. On September 12, 1923, the paper reported that 18,063 yellow bus passengers had been served at Pahaska. In addition, an average of 150 other tourists had been served meals, giving Pahaska an approximate patronage of 29,313 people for the 1923 season. Among these guests had been Governor William H. Ross and his wife, whose letter of appreciation to Files for Pahaska's hospitality was printed in the newspaper.[10]

The bonanza year of 1923 provided Jack Files with the incentive and the capital to buy Pahaska from Lulu Hall. His lease on the lodge contained an option to buy, and he exercised that option on January 9, 1924. Their mutual friend and lawyer F. V. H. Collins arranged the sale, which reputedly was for $18,000. Lulu Hall continued to live in Cody until at least 1927. She died on May 26, 1928, during a visit to Los Angeles.[11]

Files announced to the paper that he planned to make Pahaska a summer clubhouse for wealthy people, and that he had an agent in the East who had already secured 200 members. Pahaska would continue to serve meals to tourists as before, but big plans were afoot for enlarging and beautifying Pahaska. It was to be a sad irony for Jack Files that just after he had embarked upon a highly successful phase of his business career, his health began to fail. Little more than four months after buying Pahaska, Files sold it, although he continued to manage the Irma Hotel. He died suddenly at his home in Cody on February 23, 1925, at the age of fifty-three.[12]

8 | The Bizarre Case of Roscoe F. Warren

On May 13, 1924, Jack Files sold Pahaska to the Mutual Rocky Mountain Club for $22,500. In the transaction, J. Burton Warren of Rochester, New York, acted as the representative of this organization, which was composed exclusively of Masons. The purpose of the club in buying Pahaska was to establish a place where Masons and their families could hunt and fish and visit the park at a minimum of cost for service. Accommodations at Pahaska were not to be limited to club members or Masons, but were to be open to the usual tourist trade. Roscoe Francis Warren, the nephew of J. Burton Warren, was the primary organizer of the Mutual Rocky Mountain Club. The club membership consisted of from three to four hundred Masons primarily from the state of Oklahoma and Kansas City, Missouri. Roscoe Warren, a man with the rather diverse background of one-time banker in Gardiner, Montana, insurance man and player piano salesman in Kansas City, and promoter of various enterprises, was a hunter and outdoorsman who had often frequented the Cody country. From about 1918 to 1924 he had been a guest at Holm Lodge, the Nordquist Ranch, Valley Ranch, and Pahaska and had organized local hunting parties. It was at Warren's urging that the Mutual Rocky Mountain Club, of which he was general manager and treasurer, made the decision to buy Pahaska.[1]

Roscoe Warren spent the summer of 1924 at Pahaska, where the lodge experienced a busy season serving the growing number of tourists passing through the east entrance. Except for mention of a Medical-Dental Association meeting, and later of a dance, the Cody newspaper was unusually quiet about happenings at Pahaska. Warren's activities at Pahaska that summer and his return to Kansas City would, however, produce newspaper headlines and column upon column of story material for the next ten years.[2]

Ray Prante of Cody, who was operating a transfer service in 1924, drove Warren from Pahaska to Cody where Warren was to catch the train to Kansas City. Prante recalls that Warren seemed very nervous— an understandable condition, since he had been called to Kansas City by the club trustees to make an accounting of funds.[3]

W. B. Housh of Blackwell, Oklahoma, one of the trustees of the Mutual Rocky Mountain Club, had questioned Warren's handling of the club funds and had called for an audit of the books. The audit showed that Warren's personal accounts and the accounts of membership dues were badly mixed and that there was an apparent discrepancy of funds amounting to around $78,000. The trustees called Warren to Kansas City to make explanation about his use of club funds. The trustees discussed this matter in several meetings, and when Warren arrived in Kansas City, he was questioned by attorneys concerning the affairs of the club. Following these actions, several of the trustees held a meeting on October 13, 1924, in a suite of law offices in the Scarritt Building. W. B. Housh, who had initiated the investigation, was present at this meeting along with Eugene S. Briggs, secretary of the club; H. S. Tower, managing trustee of the club, and lawyers representing the club and Warren. John C. Deskin, another trustee present there, opened the meeting by reading a resolution calling for the resignation of Warren.

Warren's lawyer had cautioned Warren, who had been invited to the meeting, to stay in an adjacent room until his presence was called for in the main conference room. Warren ignored this advice and stepped into the conference room just as Deskin was reading the resolution. Shouting "It's a damnable lie!" he drew a revolver and fired five shots at Deskin. Warren then walked out into the hall and shot himself in the left chest, the bullet missing his heart and lodging under his shoulder blade. As Warren and Deskin were rushed to the hospital, crowds gathered in the streets in front, and nearby office windows were thrown open as people looked out to see what all the noise and excitement were about. By the crime standards of *The Kansas City Times,* the shooting incident was a ho-hum everyday occurrence which rated only the second page for discussion.

Neal Warren, Warren's son, had been present in the room next to the conference room where the shooting had taken place. When questioned by the police later, he said that he had taken a revolver from his father before they left for the conference. He also said that his father had been in a shooting affair in Wyoming several years earlier.[4]

As he lay in a cell ward in Kansas City Hospital, Warren told reporters that the shooting was a result of disagreements between him and Deskin over the disposition of the club's funds. He said that Housh had maligned him, and that he had used his own money in the organization of the club. Meanwhile, in another room in the same hospital, Deskin lay dying. He passed away on October 15, 1924, at the age of thirty-six. He was survived by his wife and two children, aged nine and three.[5]

On October 20 Warren was charged in criminal court with the first degree murder of John C. Deskin, President of the Deskin Automobile Company. An indictment for first degree murder by the Jackson County grand jury soon followed. Warren was held in the county jail until May 1925, when his trial began. His lawyers offered insanity as the defense, but Warren didn't help them much by interrupting his own lawyers and witnesses frequently by saying, "I'm not crazy, I tell you, I'm not crazy." In support of the insanity plea Warren's lawyers pointed out his family background, his physical appearance, his odd dress, his mannerisms. They gave evidence that his grandfather, father, uncle and cousin had committed suicide. They said his body was abnormal—one index finger was much longer than the middle digit; his ears didn't match—one was longer than the other; one side of his head was longer than the other; and the lawyers contended that nature fell short of perfection in his mental makeup as well. His attire was offered as further evidence of his insanity—he wore a kimono at home, and seemingly to emphasize his eccentricity, he wore a braid-edged black suit, wing collar, and patent leather slippers to the court room every day. As the ultimate proof that Warren was crazy, his lawyer said his client had once paid Irene Castle fifty dollars each for twenty successive dances.[6]

Despite all this bizarre evidence presented to it, the jury decided that Warren was sane when he killed Deskin. It found him guilty of second degree murder and sentenced him to fifteen years in prison. The case was appealed to the Supreme Court of Missouri, and Warren was released on bond. On December 7, 1925, while free on bond, Warren married nineteen-year-old Dorothy Decrof, who had been visiting him regularly at the county jail. In 1927 the state supreme court reversed the sentence and ordered a new trial. At the second trial in March 1928, Warren pleaded insanity and self-defense, and this time the jury found him guilty of first degree murder and sentenced him to be hanged. The date of hanging was set for June 1, 1928. Warren's lawyer again filed a notice of appeal. No bond was allowed and Warren waited in jail until June 1930 when the state supreme court again reversed his case, stating that the death sentence was too severe and that a provision for second degree murder should have been in the instruction to the jury. At the third trial, held in February 1931, Warren pleaded guilty and was sentenced to ten years in prison. In June 1934, nearly ten years after he murdered Deskin,

Warren walked away from the Missouri penitentiary a free man, paroled by Governor Guy B. Park. Warren had served about seven of those ten years in prison.[7]

That Warren was a murderer there was no doubt. But was he an embezzler, as the club trustees seemed to believe? The murder trials occupied the stage for ten years and the club never brought charges against him to recover its money. Was this lack of action tacit admission that the club could not develop a solid case against Warren, or was it merely that the Masons wanted to step as quickly as possible out of the spotlight in which the sensational shooting had placed them? To have considered embezzlement or other charges against Warren would only have afforded further embarrassment and adverse publicity to their Masonic organizations. The Masons seem to have washed their hands of Warren, a 33rd degree Mason, as soon as they could. He was expelled from Ivanhoe Lodge No. 446 in Kansas City on October 23, 1924, just ten days after the shooting.[8]

The question still remains as to what Warren was up to at Pahaska. The tangled finances of the Mutual Rocky Mountain Club shed no light on Warren's motivations. Whether he was attempting to bilk the club and assume sole control and ownership of Pahaska is a matter for conjecture. It seems clear, though, that Warren had ambitious plans for the lodge and spent a great deal of money during the summer of 1924 on horses, saddles, bridles, halters and other equipment. In Kansas City he purchased at least fifty all-leather stock saddles and had his initials, RFW, embossed in a design on the fenders. To improve the quality of Wyoming saddle horses, he bought two fine seven-gait saddle horses from horse breeders James and Mary Brock of Centralia, Missouri. One of these was Grand Duluth, a fine stallion, whose sire was a great champion; the other was Ruth, sister to Grand Duluth. These horses were shipped to Pahaska for breeding purposes. Pahaska owners in the past had always relied on concessionaires to furnish saddle horses for the lodge guests. By the end of the summer of 1924 Warren had acquired over thirty horses for Pahaska, including two Shetland ponies, Zulu, and Peaches and Cream, which he had sent out from Kansas City.

An interesting insight into Warren's personality and methods is furnished by his former daughter-in-law, Merna C. Miller. She characterized Warren as the spoiled child of a well-to-do Virginia family. He grew into manhood self-centered and fastidious, his dignified and even gracious manner masking a violent temper. His first wife, Leatha Robbins, whom he divorced, had been a queen of the New Orleans Mardi Gras. His second wife, who died about

1921, was a daughter of the socially prominent and wealthy Muehlebach family of Kansas City. This marriage may have been the source of funds for Warren's investments in Pahaska. Warren operated on a grand scale—everything had to be perfect. He lavished money on fancy ropes, halters, saddles and bridles, and fine gaited horses for Pahaska, and he overextended himself. He was accused by the Masonic club of misappropriating money. Mrs. Miller suggests he may not have been dishonest but was merely a big spender.[9]

From his jail cell in Jackson County, Missouri, Roscoe F. Warren directed his uncle, J. Burton Warren, who had been the Masons' principal agent in the purchase of Pahaska, to transfer the former's rights in the lodge and associated properties to Donald B. Warren of Rochester, New York. The relationship between the two is not known; D. B. Warren may have been another uncle of Roscoe Warren. In any case, Warren's financial interest in the Mutual Rocky Mountain Club, whatever it may have amounted to, was duly transferred to D. B. Warren on October 23, 1924.[10]

Wilkinson Era Begins, 1925

The Wymozoca (Wyoming-Missouri-Oklahoma) Realty Company was incorporated on December 3, 1924 in Kansas City, Missouri, for the purpose of buying, selling or leasing tracts of land suitable for hunting and fishing or other recreational activities. The amount of capital stock was $50,000, which was the exact amount needed to purchase the properties of the Mutual Rocky Mountain Club. These properties and their listed values were as follows: Pahaska, $25,000; Chapaton Cabin, $3,400; Boulder Lodge (White Bear or Camp Kerwan) on Boulder River, Sweetgrass County, Contact, Montana, $8,000; Jones Creek campsite leasehold, three and one-half miles north of Pahaska, $2,000; camp equipment including horses, $1,000; trophies, $1,000; office equipment at Kansas City, $600. The directors were Eugene S. Briggs of Kansas City, Missouri and Okmulgee, Oklahoma; and Willard Francis Wilkinson and Dale R. Nuss of Kansas City.[1]

J. Burton Warren of Rochester, New York established a temporary residence in Kansas City beginning in the fall of 1924 to aid his nephew with legal matters connected with the shooting affair. Also, he was there as the president of the Mutual Rocky Mountain Club to resolve the matter of the disposition of the club's interest in Pahaska and other properties. Along with E. S. Briggs, who was the secretary of the club, J. Burton Warren also became involved with the Wymozoca Realty Company. Briggs was made the secretary of this company and J. Burton Warren became vice-president. Thus, all the officers of the Mutual Rocky Mountain Club except Roscoe F. Warren, the former treasurer, who was in jail, had become members and officers of the Wymozoca Company. Willard F. Wilkinson was the president.

The background to the formation of the Wymozoca Realty Company began with the acquaintance of Eugene S. Briggs with Dale R. Nuss. Dale Nuss was associated with his father, Willis E. Nuss, in the Nuss Oil Burner Manufacturing Company in Kansas City. He had become friends with Briggs and this led to Nuss's obtaining a job at Pahaska during the summer of 1924, when Roscoe Warren was managing the lodge. Nuss then returned to Kansas City in the late summer of 1924 to work for his father again. It was then that he met Willard F. Wilkinson.

Willard "Bill" F. Wilkinson was a 1922 graduate in business administration from the University of Missouri. He spent a year of postgraduate study in business at the University of Chicago and then married Jessie R. Brenizer on November 17, 1923. Wilkinson worked in a Kansas City bank for a few months in 1923 and early 1924 and then left for employment as a salesman with the Nuss Oil Burner Manufacturing Company. Wilkinson became acquainted with Dale Nuss when the latter returned to Kansas City from Wyoming. Both were working at the Nuss Oil Burner business when the shooting incident occurred on October 13. Dale Nuss correctly assumed that in the aftermath of the tragedy, the Masons would be interested in selling Pahaska. He discussed Pahaska with Wilkinson and convinced him that it was an excellent business opportunity. Bill Wilkinson was only twenty-three years old and was not wealthy, but his modest assets could be expanded greatly from the substantial inheritance his mother, Alberta E. Wilkinson of Stewartsville, Missouri, had received from the estate of her deceased husband.

Eugene S. Briggs and J. Burton Warren, who were in Kansas City, also played roles in interesting Wilkinson in Pahaska. J. Burton Warren socialized with Bill and Jessie Wilkinson, and along with Briggs and Nuss, helped to organize the Wymozoca Realty Company. Wilkinson was made the president of the company, presumably more in recognition of the substantial funds he could contribute than for his experience. The Wymozoca Company used its funds to buy out all the interests of the Mutual Rocky Mountain Club in Pahaska and Chapaton Cabin except those interests held by J. Burton Warren and Donald B. Warren. It also bought the club's interests in the trophies and equipment at Pahaska as well as the Jones Creek camp leasehold and Boulder Lodge in Montana.[2]

The Warrens held the majority interest in Pahaska when it opened for tourists in the summer of 1925. J. Burton Warren arrived in Cody early in May preparing to undertake his duties as general manager of Pahaska. Since he was required to be in Kansas City and Rochester at various times during the summer, Warren hired Dale Nuss to be resident manager in 1925—a position he would hold through 1927.[3]

Bill Wilkinson and his wife drove from Kansas City to Pahaska, arriving there in June 1925. Wilkinson wanted to find out about Pahaska firsthand before committing any more funds to the project.

He spent the summer there checking out the operations, and liking what he saw, determined to buy it. Records in the Park County Courthouse show that on August 15, 1925, J. Burton Warren and Donald B. Warren sold their interests in Pahaska and all its equipment and horses, and Chapaton Cabin, to the Wymozoca Realty Company.[4]

Briggs, Nuss and James S. Summers, a Kansas City lawyer, each owned some stock in the company—but Wilkinson was the majority stockholder. In anticipation of buying out the Warrens, Wilkinson had obtained a loan from his mother in May 1924, in the name of the Wymozoca Company.Mrs. Wilkinson had accepted as collateral for her loan whatever interest the company had or might acquire in Pahaska. These new funds were then used to consummate the purchase of Pahaska in August 1925.

This loan, dated May 1925, was due one year later. On June 1, 1926, the loan had not been repaid and was overdue. The company had been making some expensive improvements at Pahaska and apparently didn't have the funds for repayment. Alberta Wilkinson then served a notice of default and on June 24 she foreclosed upon Pahaska, leaving the Wymozoca Company with no further claims on the lodge. On November 5, 1927, she bought Chapaton Cabin from the Wymozoca Company.[5]

Why Mrs. Wilkinson chose to foreclose the mortgage instead of extending the loan period is not clear. Perhaps she and her son had decided to squeeze out the other stockholders and obtain sole control of the lodge. Since neither the Wymozoca Company nor any of its members took legal action to recover any losses, it appears that all of the stockholders recovered their investments. The sale of Boulder Lodge and Chapaton Cabin would, perhaps, have produced enough funds to accomplish this. Moreover, Wilkinson remained on friendly terms with the stockholders and, in fact, retained Dale Nuss as manager for the summers of 1926 and 1927. With the sale or loss of all its investment assets, the Wymozoca Realty Company had ceased to exist by 1927.

Alberta Wilkinson at first impression appeared to be an unlikely candidate for active participation in the management of Pahaska. A heavyset, gray-haired woman, who had spent most of her adult life as wife to a prosperous Missouri stock grower and farmer, she was in the mid-1920s a widow with sufficient funds to live out her life comfortably. She chose instead to support her son's participation in the Wymozoca Company, and then later to become personally involved in the day-to-day operations of Pahaska almost to the end of her life. In the maneuvering which led to her acquisition of control

Alberta E. Wilkinson, owner of Pahaska, 1926-46. Photo courtesy Jessie B. Kensel, Ellensburg, Washington.

over Pahaska, she emerged as a shrewd and cautious businesswoman. From the first summer in 1926 when she began working at Pahaska, until 1946 when she sold the lodge, she maintained a constant vigil over her investment—providing an essential balance wheel to her able and intelligent, but often erratic son with whom she shared management for twenty years. It was her money that was used to buy Pahaska, and the title to the property was always in her name, despite frequent references by Cody people and by Cody newspapers to Bill Wilkinson as owner of Pahaska.

The complicated evolution of the management structure at Pahaska which began in 1924 with the nefarious Roscoe F. Warren was finally resolved when Alberta Wilkinson obtained full ownership of the lodge in 1926. Against this background Pahaska continued to function successfully as a resort operation. The lively, confused and individualistic 1920s were prosperous years. The invention of the automobile and the development of mass production had provided almost everyone with a car. Hard-surfaced roads spread across the countryside with startling speed, and in the 1920s hundreds of thousands of people invaded the roads in their own cars to visit vacation spots all over America. Statistics from the National Park

Service reveal that Yellowstone National Park was a favorite destination for the auto tourist, although the numbers of those who arrived at the park entrances by rail remained significant.

A record was established at the east entrance on July 5, 1924 for the largest motor travel on a single day, when 224 cars carrying 696 people entered the park. A total of 9,930 cars went through this entrance in the 1924 season—more than through any other entrance. These gains in auto traffic were made in spite of the handicaps imposed by the narrow road through Shoshone Canyon and the steep climb up Sylvan Pass. Many tourists were thrilled by the scenic beauty of the road, but were frightened enough by the obstacles to warn others not to take the Cody Road to Yellowstone National Park. An important improvement was made to the road in June, 1925, when a double-width road as far as the dam and a concrete arch bridge at the entrance of Shoshone Canyon were opened to the public. After Miss Jane Garlow, granddaughter of the late Col. Cody, had christened the new bridge with a bottle of DeMaris spring water, the superintendent of Yellowstone National Park, Horace M. Albright, expressed the hope that the new wide road would help to eliminate the fears of travelers. The improvements may have helped to improve the reputation of the Cody Road, since the number of cars entering the east entrance jumped from 11,686 cars in 1925 to 15,827 in 1926, with this entrance maintaining its lead in auto traffic over other entrances to 1928. Improvements to the Cody Road continued through the years. In 1927 the road beyond the dam was widened, making virtually the entire Shoshone Canyon route a two-lane road. *The Cody Enterprise* summed up the new construction this way: "No more will the tourist get a cold chill in rounding the narrow curves or negotiating the steep grades as he did on the old route through the Shoshone Canyon, and the ease with which the canyon may be negotiated will make it many more times interesting to the timid motorist." The canyon road may have produced chills, but the worst and most difficult stretch of the Cody Road was in Sylvan Pass. In 1930 a new road was completed through the pass, reducing the grade and eliminating the old corkscrew bridge. The hairpin turns and steep climb to the top of the pass were also eliminated—much to every traveler's relief, but especially to eastern and midwestern drivers unused to the mountain grades and narrow passages.[6]

The golden twenties and vistas of unlimited tourists coming up the road helped to inspire the creation of a number of new dude ranches on the North Fork. Among these were the Red Star Camp of Henry Dahlem and J. H. Vogel; Elephant Head Lodge, operated

Willard F. "Bill" Wilkinson, manager of Pahaska, 1927-1946 and son. Photo courtesy Jessie B. Kensel, Ellensberg, Washington.

by Mr. and Mrs. Harry W. Thurston; and W. G. Sherwin's Trail Shop. Those ranches established before 1920 and still operating in the 1920s included Holm Lodge, owned by Billy Howell and Mary Shawver; the Fred Morris Ranch; the Jim Creek Heights Ranch—established originally by Peter and Lawrence Nordquist, and operated in the 1920s as the P Bar P Ranch by Peter Nordquist and Albert G. Wilkinson. In 1930 S. S. Kuentzel and his wife Olive Fell acquired Nordquist's interest in the P Bar P and it was incorporated as the Four Bear Ranch. Other ranches which continued to operate in the 1920s were Blackwater Camp, owned by Mrs. Anna B. Rumsey until 1930 when it was sold to Mr. and Mrs. Tex Wisdom; and Absaroka Lodge started by Mr. and Mrs. Earl Crouch and operated until the 1920s by various partners, including Earl Martin, Clarence Wood and Earl Hayner.[7]

Increasing numbers of tourists prompted the Yellowstone Park Camps Company in 1924 to build Sylvan Pass Lodge just inside the park at the east entrance. The yellow buses of Yellowstone Park Transportation Company continued for a few years to stop at Pahaska for meals, but only on an irregular basis. Their regularly scheduled lunch stop was at the new lodge. Bill Wilkinson complained to the National Park Service that Sylvan Pass Lodge provided an unnecessary and inefficient duplication of services. Competition from the new lodge would obviously reduce the volume of business at Pahaska. Anything that hurt Pahaska also affected Cody businesses furnishing goods and services to the lodge. Moreover, Codyites had from the beginning consistently supported the building of the Cody Road with political and financial support as well as unpaid volunteer labor on the road. The completion of the road and the opening of the east entrance to Yellowstone National Park was a boon to Cody, but it also contributed in an important way to the overall development of the park as a great recreational resource. Cody people believed then that park authorities owed them some consideration on matters affecting Cody's economy. Many Cody people had been resentful of the creation of what they called transportation, camp and hotel monopolies in the park in 1917 and were sensitized more than ever to park actions which affected them. The operation of Sylvan Pass Lodge would hardly have devastated Cody's economy—but a principle was involved here, and Wilkinson got unexpected Cody support in his bid to shut down the lodge. Sylvan Pass Lodge was finally closed and torn down in the early 1930s—partly in response to local pressures and partly because the lodge was not well-maintained.[8]

The management at Pahaska responded to the surge of tourists in the mid-1920s with a modernization program. During 1925 J. Burton Warren arranged for the installation of a new sewage system at Pahaska. A large septic tank was buried across the Cody Road from the lodge. This was used for sewage disposal until 1958 when it was replaced by an oxidation pond built adjacent to the North Fork River.

In 1926, when the Wilkinsons assumed full control of Pahaska, they instructed manager Dale Nuss to continue the program of

Pahaska, 1926. The roadside appearance of Pahaska was changed by the new Wilkinson management with the removal of the porch screens and the erection of new stone entry posts, and a new stone chimney for the lodge. Photo courtesy Jessie B. Kensel, Ellensburg, Washington.

Lobby of Pahaska Lodge, c. 1926. Photo courtesy Jessie B. Kensel, Ellensburg, Washington.

improvements. Nuss installed a gasoline-powered water pump just over the river bank from the laundry house. Water was pumped from the North Fork up to the old wooden water tank on the hill. This replaced the old system, first established in 1910, of piping water directly from Middle Creek to the tank. There were no cabins above Pahaska on the North Fork, so the purity of the water was never in question. At the direction of the Wilkinsons, Nuss removed the screens which had enclosed the porches around the lodge since 1910. Nuss also razed the old dance pavilion, which had been, since its construction in 1911, a major entertainment center at Pahaska. In 1926, the pavilion was broken down and rotting from exposure to the heavy snows of a decade-and-a-half of winters.[9]

In an effort to improve the roadside appearance of Pahaska, the Wilkinsons removed the plain wooden posts which framed the entry road leading to the front door of the lodge. These were replaced in 1926 by two massive concrete pillars embedded with large stones. Mounted on top of these six-foot-high pillars were large white glass globes imprinted with the likeness of Buffalo Bill. The masons who completed this job also removed the old metal chimney, which emerged from the roof of the lodge, and in its place constructed a new chimney of concrete and stone. The stone entry pillars were replaced in the late 1930s by log entry posts, but the stone chimney is in place today.

In 1927 Bill Wilkinson ordered a new water-powered electrical generator from Cody distributor S. P. Van Arsdall. A diesel-powered generator had provided electricity for Pahaska for many years, but it was too expensive to operate day and night. Wilkinson wanted to attract the auto tourist to Pahaska by keeping the lights on all night on the principal roadside buildings. Also, he needed a cheaper source of electricity for the operation of various electrical implements and for lighting the lodge and other buildings. The water-powered generator answered the need for a cheap electrical source, because once it was installed it operated almost without cost. Mr. Van Arsdall installed the new electric light plant beside Middle Creek about a mile above Pahaska. The hydroelectric plant was driven by a Fitz water wheel with a sixteen-foot shaft. A 6,000-watt generator was belted to the shaft. Water was piped downstream from Middle Creek into a large concrete basin which acted as a holding tank and maintained a constant flow of water. At this point, water flowed over the water wheel, turning the shaft connected to the generator. Occasionally, debris from Middle Creek would stop the water wheel and the lights would go out at Pahaska. When these blackouts occurred, employees would take it in stride with the customary explanation, "Fish stuck in the light plant again!" Despite a few problems, the water wheel ran day and night during the summer season and furnished Pahaska with electrical power for over twenty years.[10]

Dale Nuss resigned his position as resident manager at Pahaska in August 1927. Nuss had been an energetic and competent manager, but Bill Wilkinson, who had shared management responsibilities with Nuss, felt ready to take full charge of the operations. His mother, Alberta Wilkinson, had assumed more of the load in hiring and supervising the help at Pahaska, registering guests at the lodge, and even cooking and working in the store. Dale Nuss was no longer needed at Pahaska in a managerial capacity, so he left to become a high school vocational teacher and athletic coach in Okmulgee, Oklahoma. He was hired there by his friend and former stockholder in Pahaska, Eugene S. Briggs, who was superintendent of the Oklahoma school. Nuss never lost his love for Pahaska and the Yellowstone area. Every year he returned to Wyoming with parties of Oklahoma boys or girls for horseback tours of Yellowstone National Park. He outfitted his groups with horses and supplies at Cody or Pahaska and rode into the park to visit points of interest.[11]

Between about 1920 and the onset of the depression in the early 1930s, the Valley Ranch on the South Fork also sponsored boys' and girls' horseback tours of Yellowstone National Park. Large parties of boys and girls from eastern schools were assembled and transported to Cody in special Pullman cars. From there they would be taken to Valley Ranch where they would be outfitted for the trip. The typical pattern of operation was for the respective boys' and girls' parties to leave one day apart. On July 4, 1923, for instance, a party consisting of seventy girls,under the guidance of A. C. Newton, left Cody for the park. The next day, fifty-six boys left under Clarence Linn. These large processions followed different routes into the park, but very often went up the Cody Road where automobile traffic was still light enough so as not to pose a serious problem. In addition to the boys and girls, the party of 1923 included twenty-five men on the working staff, 100 head of saddle horses, thirty-six team horses and nine freight and cook wagons. These large groups of riders would eventually arrive at Pahaska, where they would buy a large amount of groceries and possibly eat a meal at the lodge. Then they would continue up the road on the forty-to fifty-day round trip into the park.[12]

10 Pahaska in the 1930s

Until 1931, Bill Wilkinson and his family returned to Missouri to spend the winter. For most of the rest of the 1930s the Wilkinsons moved into Cody for the winter with the closing of the tourist season. Late in 1929, while he was wintering in Stewartsville, Missouri, Wilkinson hired three local men to drive a truckload of supplies to Pahaska. When they arrived they were to join other workmen in the construction of a new store.

Several years earlier Wilkinson had converted a guest cabin into a grocery store. This little store, located on the west end of the row of guest cabins facing the Cody Road, was conveniently located to serve the needs of passing travelers and campers. A limited lunch of sandwiches and soft drinks, as well as groceries and sundries, was available to tourists.

By 1929 these services were inadequate. Wilkinson procured building materials in Cody and ordered peeled construction logs from Henry Dahlem's nearby mill at Red Star Camp. In April 1930, the three young Missourians, Leo F. Urban, Merle Spencer and Charley Kemp, and others, began erecting a new larger store about twenty to thirty feet west of the small store, which in turn was converted back into a guest cabin. The new log store housed a dining room which ran its full length, and a grocery counter on one side where large amounts of groceries, photographic supplies, post cards, and Indian curios were stocked. A kitchen and walk-in cellar were later built on the end of the store. A larger proportion of tourists camped out in the twenties and thirties than in the later decades, and the new Pahaska store enjoyed a substantial trade in groceries. Before the store kitchen was built, food was prepared in the lodge kitchen and brought to the store, where it was kept warm in a steam table.[1]

Clytie Williams of Cody, who worked at Pahaska from 1927 to 1937 recalls that hamburgers were unknown. The most popular sandwich was made with home-baked ham. A "Dutch Lunch Plate" for $1.00 with beer was a good seller. Liquor was available by the bottle. Later, steaks and somewhat more elaborate meals were served. In addi-

Pahaska Lodge dining room, c. 1930. This dining room and the guest rooms in the second story above were built onto the back of Pahaska Lodge in 1921 and torn down in 1963. Photo courtesy Jessie B. Kensel, Ellensburg, Washington.

tion to tourists, road crews on Sylvan Pass and the Cody Road stopped in for meals.

A lunch had been available in the lodge dining room for years. It was served family style—all you could eat for $1.00. After the store kitchen was built, breakfast and lunch were eliminated from the meal service at the lodge and were available only at the store. The lodge dining room continued to serve dinner until about 1939 when it was closed permanently for food service. In 1940 the dining room was converted into a Buffalo Bill Museum as an advertising device to attract tourists to Pahaska. Fred H. Garlow, son of early Pahaska managers Fred and Irma Garlow, operated the museum, which contained some trophies and other memorabilia of his grandfather, Col. Cody.[2]

The new Pahaska store also offered some recreational diversion in the form of slot machines, placed there by a Frannie, Wyoming gambler who was known as Diamond Dick. Diamond Dick's big lavender Cadillac was a familiar sight in the Big Horn Basin, where he plied his slot machine business. Clytie Williams said that she emptied the slot machines every night and the nickels, dimes and quarters they yielded during the depression years would likely exceed the store's receipts on any given day. The Wilkinsons got a percentage of the slot machine earnings.

In the nomenclature of the resort and dude ranch business of the time, guests were called "dudes," ranch and resort owners and guides were "dude wranglers," and the men who cared for the horses were "horse wranglers." Summer employees were "savages"— seemingly an inappropriate name for the many fine people, including students, teachers, and others who were temporary help. Clytie Williams, a year-round employee, assisted Alberta Wilkinson in supervising the female employees who had to be ready and able to work anywhere at anything that had to be done. This included being a waitress, maid, cook, laundress, or salesperson. Occasionally the girls working in the store would have to pump gas at the nearby garage. Among the female savages of the early 1930s were Edith Baker and Della Ballard, who eventually were married respectively to Missourians Charley Kemp and Leo Urban. Others included Ethel Thrasher, a Cody schoolteacher, Dorothy Stark, Minnie Martin, Mary Corder, Clara Wasden, Margaret Cornell, Helen McNiven, Mabel Baker, and Clara Myres. Their pay ranged between $35.00 and $45.00 a month, and board and room were provided. Male employees—horse wranglers, mechanics, woodcutters, and handymen received from $50.00 to $90.00.

Male and female employees were housed in separate bunkhouses located behind the lodge. These buildings had been built about 1914, and had been used then for overflow guests from the lodge, as well as for employees. The bunkhouses were crudely built with vertically placed, unpeeled slab boards. They were not insulated and had no bathrooms. None of the four guest cabins along the Cody Road had bathrooms. In fact, the only guest cabin on the entire grounds with the luxury of a bathroom was the Honeymoon Cabin built by the Wilkinsons in the early 1930s on the hill behind the garage. Edith Baker Kemp, an employee during the summers of 1929 and 1930, recalls staying in one of the two bedrooms opening on the porch on the left side of the lodge. The cook usually slept in a room above the lodge dining room. Clytie Williams and her husband also spent one summer above the dining room. She remembers their room as being uncomfortably hot from the heat coming up from the big round stove in the dining room. The next summer, as permanent employees, they were accorded the relative luxury of moving into a two-room bunkhouse behind the lodge.

Hot water, as well as bathrooms, were at a premium at Pahaska. The large wood stove in the lodge kitchen had water tanks attached to it. The water from these tanks was circulated around the firebox and furnished hot water for the kitchen. Guests in the cabins could heat water on their little wood stoves. In 1930 Charley Kemp, all-around handyman, mechanic and electrician, supervised the construction of an outdoor furnace made of mortar, bricks and stones. It was located on the right side of the lodge kitchen between the kitchen and bathhouse. A large metal tank was propped up on a frame next to it. Cold water was piped from the kitchen into the tank and then piped into the coil around the interior of the furnace. The hot water produced was then drawn off through another pipe back into the kitchen as a supplementary source of water there. Hot water was also piped from the furnace to the bathhouse lying on its other side.

Pahaska was heated exclusively by wood in the period covered by this study. There was a big wood cook stove in the lodge kitchen, one in the laundry (used just for heating) and another in the store kitchen. There was a large round stove in the lodge dining room, small stoves in all the cabins and bunkhouses, the fireplace in the lodge, and the outside furnace. Pahaska had an enormous woodpile in those days and it was Bill (Big Bill) Southworth's job to get up very early every morning and start the fires in the furnace and in the two kitchen woodstoves.[3]

In 1915 Gus Holm of Cody became the first concessionaire to offer auto repair service at Pahaska's new log garage. He was followed by others down to the middle 1920s, when A. J. Melvin was the last garageman to receive the concession. By 1927 Bill Wilkinson was aware that there was enough business from the thousands of cars then coming up the Cody Road annually to justify assuming the garage operation himself. That year he hired Ralph H. Cox, a competent mechanic, as his garage manager. Bill Bracken and Charlie Hayner, both good mechanics, also worked in the garage assisted by Charley Kemp. Tourists who had auto trouble at Pahaska were fortunate to find an excellent repair service there. Sometimes the outcome was unfortunate if parts had to be ordered from Billings or Denver and the time loss and additional expense meant that the tourist could not continue his trip into the park. For most of the period from the middle 1920s through the 1930s gas was sold at 39 cents a gallon. Such large quantities were sold during the tourist season that Charley Kemp had to drive the gas truck into Cody every day to replenish the supply.[4]

There were about thirty-five horses at Pahaska which could be rented by tourists for rides around the area. A permit from the Forest Service allowed the horses to graze freely during the night on the pastures near Pahaska. Melvin C. McGee, who worked as a horse wrangler at Pahaska during the summers of 1927, 1928 and 1929, recalls rounding up the horses and herding them into the corrals for daytime use. Vic Redding, Dell McNiven and Roy Glasgow also worked as horse wranglers during the 1930s. In the fall the horses might be used for hunting trips, but before winter set in they were driven to winter pastures in the lower North Fork Valley or on the South Fork of the Shoshone River.[5]

Pahaska was located in the midst of a forest high in the mountains. The area was the natural habitat of a wide variety of small furred animals and big game. Moose could be seen nearly every morning feeding in a swamp across the river from the lodge. Deer and elk grazed in the nearby forest pastures and bear wandered through Pahaska's grounds as casually as tourists.

The garbage at Pahaska, including an occasional dead horse, was hauled to an open dump on the hill above the Club House. At night, bears came to feed on whatever had been left. This solved the problem of garbage disposal and kept the bears satisfied. The bears could be nuisances at times when they tried to break into buildings to get food or when they frightened Pahaska's guests. On one occasion in 1938 Bill Wilkinson remarked that "we have at least twenty-five bears wandering around here all the time. It's awful—you can't walk out of a cabin at night without bumping into one. Most of them seem to be black, which makes them especially hard to see in the dark." By this time the old dump on the hill had been closed and a new garbage incinerator set up on the other side of the horse corrals. This new location proved to be a bad one, since wherever there was garbage there would be bears. One night, Wilkinson relates, his men heard a terrible commotion over at the corrals. There they found a 400-pound bear standing in the middle with a little nipper of a bear chasing the horses around in a wide circle. "The big bear looked just like a circus ring-master," said Pahaska Bill. "We popped him with a shotgun and both of them left."[6]

The bear problem was exacerbated by the park's policy of deporting bad bears. Bears that started scratching and biting too many tourists, or bears that did too much damage at campgrounds were trapped and put in a cage. When enough undesirable bears were collected, rangers hauled them to one of the park's entrances and set them free. Many of the candy-loving bears quickly galloped right back into the park, but others began looking for food in their new home and wandered down the road to Pahaska. Bill Wilkinson discouraged these furry non-paying travelers with buckshot, and they kept moving on down the road. Henry Dahlem at Red Star Camp was no more accommodating, and the bear migration continued down to Holm Lodge. Billy Howell also had a shotgun so the poor bears, weary of inhospitality, moved on down the river to Earl Hayner's Absaroka Lodge. Earl didn't welcome bears either, so if Tex Wisdom greeted them with lead pellets at Blackwater Camp, the migration might be put in reverse. Back in the park the bears could at least get respect and fawning attention from tourists—and most important, food.[7]

Since 1906, when E. S. Hoopes stayed at the lodge all winter, Pahaska had winter caretakers to see that the place was not robbed or damaged. Most of the time heavy snow on the road kept traffic to a minimum so that vandalism was not a real problem. During four successive winters, from 1930 to 1934, Clytie Williams and her first husband, Carl Wagoner, were winter caretakers at Pahaska, as well as being regular summer employees. Clytie recalls that there was much more to do than just watch the place. Enormous quantities of wood had to be cut during the winter to keep Pahaska's many stoves heated throughout all of the next year. In the fall the men would go out into the woods and fell trees and haul the logs to Pahaska. There they would be sawed into short lengths. It was Carl's and Clytie's responsibility when winter came to cut up those sawed logs into proper sizes and lengths to meet the dimensions of the various stoves and fireplaces at Pahaska. Clytie said that she and Carl had to work every third day throughout the winter in order to produce fifty to eighty cords of wood.

Another winter job for Clytie and Carl was to shovel the snow off part of the lodge roof. The front part of the lodge on the south side did not have enough pitch to shed the snow easily, so shoveling was required. Chapaton Cabin was the only other building at Pahaska that had to have its roof cleaned off periodically in the winter.

Electrical refrigeration was not used at Pahaska in the 1920s and 1930s, so putting up ice in the winter was another chore. When the ice had frozen about a foot thick on the river it was sawed by hand into chunks. It was then stored in the ice house between thick layers of sawdust. Pahaska employees joined men from other lodges on the North Fork in the task of cutting ice. When everyone had enough, the team of horses which pulled the ice wagons were driven to the Wapiti area or perhaps to the South Fork to winter there with the rest of the Pahaska horses.

During the long winter months Carl Wagoner had time to set out traps and earn extra income from the pelts of the marten, red

Porch of the Pahaska store, 1930. From left to right are Pahaska employees Edith Baker Kemp, Della Ballard Urban, Ethel Thrasher and Clytie Wagoner Williams. Photo courtesy Clytie Williams, Cody, Wyoming.

fox, coyote, and badger which he trapped. The Wilkinsons had arranged for winter camps to be established at locations north of Pahaska along Crow Creek and Red Creek. Before winter, tents and stoves were set up at these locations. During the winter Carl and someone else—since it would be too risky to go out alone—would travel by snowshoe to one of these camps. Roy Glasgow, a guide and horse wrangler at Pahaska, would often be Carl's companion. They would usually stay out three days setting and checking the trap lines, and then return to the caretaker's cabin at Pahaska. These trapping expeditions were generally very successful. A good marten skin brought $30.00 to $75.00, with the other pelts bringing lesser amounts.

When the snowfall became heavy, Carl and Clytie would leave their car several miles down the road at Holm Lodge. From there they could usually drive down to Cody for supplies. This provided some opportunity to visit other people, but their social contacts were mostly limited to close neighbors. They might ski or snowshoe to the east entrance station to see ranger Ted Ogston and his wife Helen or travel by the same means down to Holm Lodge to visit Chris and Winifred Pike, the winter caretakers.[8]

In September 1934, while on a hunting trip above Pahaska, Carl became seriously ill from complications of stomach ulcers. Bill Wilkinson and other hunters improvised a stretcher and carried Carl sixteen miles down to Pahaska. Though he was rushed to a Cody hospital, it was too late to save him. Carl had been a well-liked and respected man, and his death was a great loss to Pahaska and to the entire Cody community.[9]

The beginning of the Great Depression of the 1930s was reflected in the reduction of visitors to Yellowstone National Park. The number of visiting tourists had climbed steadily over the years to 260,697 in 1929. In 1930 this figure dropped to 227,901. Correspondingly, the peak number of tourists entering through the east entrance reached 81,305 in 1929 and then dropped back to 69,716 in 1930. By 1934, probably due to the stimulating effects of President Franklin D. Roosevelt's New Deal programs, there was a noticeable increase in the total number of travelers visiting the park. This improvement continued unabated until 1942, when the impact of World War II again brought a precipitous decline in numbers of travelers.[10]

The depression of the 1930s and decreasing numbers of travelers brought hard times to the resorts and dude ranches on the Cody Road. Billy Howell and Mary Shawver at Holm Lodge admitted that 1932 was a bad year for them, but they were more hopeful about 1933. Clytie Williams, who usually totaled up the day's receipts at Pahaska, noted that on many days the receipts didn't cover the pay of the employees. Bill Wilkinson found it painful to tell people they weren't needed. In 1932 he had hired a number of people from out of state when he realized that the depression was reducing his volume of business. He informed the newly-arrived employees that they could stay at lower wages or go home. Every one of them stayed. At the bottom of the depression a year or so later, Pahaska's work crew was reduced to a skeleton force. Clytie and Carl and a handful of employees worked along with Bill and Jess Wilkinson and his mother, Alberta, to serve the needs of their guests.[11]

In 1932, Yellowstone National Park received only 157,624 visitors, the lowest number recorded during the depression. In 1933 park officials responded to this dramatic decrease by closing the hotels at Mammoth and Lake Yellowstone and by operating Old Faithful and Canyon lodges with only a small number of rooms open for service. These facilities were opened again in 1934 and remained open through the remainder of the depression.

Even after 1934, when every year showed a healthy increase

in the numbers of travelers through the east entrance, business at Pahaska remained in the doldrums. The store did a large business in selling groceries, and gas sold well at the garage pumps. But tourists did not, as in earlier years, come in droves for meal service and lodging. In the early days, the traveler who took the road to the park with his own wagon and horses and supplies, including a tent, was called a "sage brusher." The new sage brusher of the 1930s drove an automobile and on the running board carried his tent, blankets and other supplies. This economizing, almost self-sufficient tourist needed only gas and a few groceries to keep him going. Only during a heavy rain would the rooms and cabins at Pahaska be full—even a sage brusher could only take so much!

11 An Era of Transition, 1939-1946

From a low of 49,276 visitors entering through the east entrance in 1932 to a new high of 139,213 in 1937, business gradually began to improve along the Cody Road. Through most of the 1930s the east entrance continued to be the most popular entrance for auto tourists. The number of cars entering the east entrance had always been a fairly reliable indicator of the volume of business at Pahaska during any given summer. From the time of its opening as a hotel in 1904 to the late 1930s, Pahaska's entire yearly receipts were derived from its operations during the three months or so of the summer season.[1]

Beginning in 1939, Pahaska and other resorts and dude ranches along the Cody Road began to consider the extension of their active business season into the winter. This new development was based on an investigation conducted in January 1939 by several skiing enthusiasts from Cody. This group, consisting of John Vogel, Dr. U. Sloniger, Roy Holm, and Shoshone Forest Supervisor A. A. McCutchen, drove up the North Fork Valley to look for a good winter sports area. They concluded that a winter sports area could not be established east of Holm Lodge because of insufficient snow. John Vogel reported that "behind Dahlem's Red Star camp on Grinnell Creek the snow is much heavier than down below. The best conditions we found lay above the junction of the Northfork and the Middlefork." Supervisor McCutchen added, "What we need is a general ski course—a place to provide sport for the entire community. It should provide gentle slopes for children and beginners, steeper slopes and possibly a ski jump for advanced skiers and experts."[2]

The initiative to establish a winter sports area on the Cody Road was taken the following month, in February 1939, by Henry Dahlem and his sons Clarence and Henry. They had been inspired by a successful winter sports carnival they had witnessed near Bozeman, Montana, and had decided to sponsor a similar event at their Red Star Camp for Big Horn Basin skiers and tobogganists. They established two ski runs and a toboggan run, and the newly organized

Shoshone Alpine Club of Cody established an "up-ski." An up-ski was a motor-driven cable which skiers grabbed, and were whisked up the mountainside to begin their runs without the trouble of having to climb. The Dahlems prepared a number of cabins and some rooms in the main lodge, and Mrs. Dahlem planned a free lunch for the Sunday carnival. This successful event launched winter sports in the upper North Fork Valley on the road to becoming a significant recreational and business activity.[3]

In a meeting the following September, the Shoshone Alpine Club agreed to leave the up-ski at Red Star Camp. The club also unanimously agreed to plan a second tow for a new skiing grounds at Pahaska. Bill Wilkinson responded to this opportunity to extend the operation of Pahaska into the winter by planning a new ski lodge. Rooms in the old Pahaska lodge were being used only occasionally for overflow guests during the late 1930s. These rooms would not be adequate for winter guests. When Jack Files added one men's and one women's bathroom in the lodge in 1921, his guests were undoubtedly impressed by the accommodations of the lodge. The guests of the late thirties, however, had become accustomed to more amenities than the lodge could offer. There were no locks on the room doors. The partitions between the rooms were merely sawed boards, and the noise level could become annoying. Moreover, there was no central heating system which could supply heat to its thirty upstairs rooms. Warmth drifting up from the fireplace and the dining room stove could not suffice in the winter.

By early October 1939, the foundations for the two-story ski lodge had been completed. Beautiful old cast-iron bedsteads with Victorian designs had been embedded in the concrete for reinforcement. While the lodge construction was underway, the Shoshone Alpine Club completed clearing the new ski course of brush and stumps and installing a 500-foot tow. The course was ready by early January 1940, but the ski lodge was not completed for use that season.[4]

The ski lodge was formally opened on November 24, 1940, and the newspaper hailed its completion as "an important step in the development of winter sports in the Cody country." The new lodge, located on the hill immediately behind the Pahaska store, was an impressive log structure ninety-four-feet long and fifty-two-feet wide. A carefully crafted stairway of native stone provided an elegant entrance to the lodge. The rustic theme of the exterior was repeated inside in log and knotty pine finishing. The main room, dotted with Navajo rugs, was normally used as a lounge—but could be cleared for a dance. At one end stood a massive stone fireplace finished with pink granite from Shoshone Canyon. The new lodge included sixteen guest rooms, all with bath, a dining room, large kitchen, private apartment for the owner, and a cocktail lounge.

At its meeting on December 3, 1940, the Shoshone Alpine Club decided to sponsor the first dance ever held at the new Pahaska ski lodge. The event, set for December 14, was to be open to the general public. At this meeting Bill Wilkinson reported that he had made extensive improvements on the Pahaska ski course, widening it and smoothing out the surface of the course. At his own expense he had installed enough additional rope to operate on the same motor an additional up-ski about 650 feet long. He said that he also planned to install electric lighting for night skiing on the course. The skiing area was located conveniently up the hill from the new lodge.[5]

Through January and February 1941, *The Cody Enterprise* carried front page stories of weekend skiing at Pahaska. On February 5, the paper reported that 400 people, the biggest crowd of winter sports fans in the history of the Cody country, had stormed Pahaska on the previous Saturday and Sunday. The crowd included people from Red Lodge, Lovell, Powell, Billings, Sheridan, Basin, and Helena. According to the paper, "The ski course looked like Times Square on election night." It added that "many visitors praised the course of the Shoshone Alpine Club, saying that its snow conditions far surpassed those of other courses in general excellence." On February 23, the Shoshone Alpine Club held its first invitational ski meet at Pahaska.[6]

The growing popularity of skiing in the Cody country led the club to support the development of a new ski course across the river from Red Star Camp. By August 1941, the work of clearing the trees had begun. Late in January 1942, Henry Coe, president of the Shoshone Alpine Club announced that the new run, called the Sleeping Giant ski course, was open for regular operation along with Pahaska's ski course. The following month the club held its annual ski meet on both ski courses.[7]

In less than three years the Shoshone Alpine Club had successfully spearheaded the development of winter sports at Pahaska and Red Star Camp. The Wilkinsons and the Dahlems had enthusiastically supported these developments, which helped to extend their business season and their profits. Pahaska in particular, with its new ski lodge, seemed to be on the threshhold of a lucrative new business in winter sports. These bright prospects were clouded, however, by the opening of World War II. Reports began to appear in the news-

Buffalo Bill Lodge at Pahaska. Manager Bill Wilkinson built this ski lodge in 1940 in an effort to promote recreational skiing at Pahaska. It burned to the ground on September 11, 1942, and was not rebuilt due to wartime material shortages. After the war an employee dormitory was built on its foundations. Photo courtesy Jessie B. Kensel, Ellensburg, Washington.

paper in 1942 about the need to share rides, to conserve tires, gas, and cars. Actual rationing of gas and tires began to erode the number of people appearing on the ski courses. Many of the young skiers began to enter the armed forces. Americans turned to the serious business of winning the war and drastically reduced their recreational activities. The number of visitors to Yellowstone National Park dropped from 581,761 in 1941 to 191,830 in 1942, and fell to a wartime low of 64,144 in 1943.[8]

World War II pushed tourist-related businesses into another period of depression after only a brief respite from the Great Depression of the 1930s. Bill Wilkinson was soon to suffer an additional blow that would seriously handicap his efforts to develop Pahaska as a winter sports area. In the spring of 1942 the gas mangle was moved from the old log laundry house situated on the bank of the North Fork to the basement of the ski lodge. In one way this was a logical change, because the ski lodge was used as a utility building in the summer and a laundry had been established in its large drive-in basement. In another way the move was completely illogical, because the old gas mangle had a long history of catching on fire. The inside of the laundry house was blackened from fires caused by the malfunctioning of the mangle.

Tom F. Trimmer of Cody, who worked at Pahaska in 1942, recalls that in the moving process the mangle was jolted and some of its pipe fittings were loosened. One day, as Trimmer was preparing to drive to Cody, Bill Wilkinson asked him to show Harry Johnson, another Pahaska employee, how to light the mangle. On this occasion on September 11, 1942, as Trimmer was lighting the mangle, it exploded. Trimmer was sprayed with gasoline, but he escaped with only superficial burns on his hand. A fire extinguisher, normally kept near the mangle, had been borrowed and not returned. The fire spread quickly through the basement until it engulfed the entire structure. Firefighters from Cody and Yellowstone Park unsuccessfully battled the blaze for five hours. The lodge was burned to the ground. Wilkinson estimated the loss at $75,000, which was only partially covered by insurance. Wartime restrictions and a shortage of building materials made it impossible to consider replacing the lodge at that time.[9]

During 1944 and 1945, the number of tourists visiting Yellowstone National Park remained well below pre-war levels. None of the park hotels, lodges or cafeterias operated in those years, and the only tourist cabins open were those at Fishing Bridge. None of the railroads serving the park delivered passengers to the various entrances, with the exception of the Northern Pacific, which operated a bus between the main line at Livingston, Montana, and the north entrance at Gardiner. These dismal developments translated into hard times for the dude ranches and resorts along the Cody Road.[10]

By late 1945 wartime rationing had ended, and for the first time in several years *The Cody Enterprise* carried a front page story about a skiing party on the Sleeping Giant ski course. The same article quoted Bill Wilkinson as saying that he planned to rebuild the ski lodge at Pahaska. This was not to be. Wilkinson lacked the financial resources to rebuild the lodge. His health had begun to fail, and his mother, who had been an unerring business partner, was in her seventies and in poor health. Moreover, Bill Wilkinson was tired of the struggle. More than half of his years at Pahaska had been spent in trying to survive through peacetime and wartime depressions in the tourist business. A few halcyon years after 1925 had provided good financial returns, but the onset of World War II severely damaged Wilkinson's hopes for expanding Pahaska's services. Large capital resources would be required for the modernization program so badly needed at Pahaska.

Wilkinson was fortunate in finding a buyer with the necessary resources. On April 2, 1946, Henry H. R. Coe of Cody bought a seventy-percent share in Pahaska. The partnership with Wilkinson was brief. Coe acquired the remaining thirty percent share on October 3, 1946. A new era in Pahaska's history had begun.[11]

Mr. and Mrs. Henry Coe had deep roots in the Cody country and were logical successors to ownership of Pahaska. They had the funds and the commitment to undertake an extensive modernization program. The two-story log addition that Jack Files had built onto the main lodge was torn off. The old laundry building, the Mystery House, the ice house, the log garage, the bunkhouses, the saddle shed and barns and other older structures were torn down or relocated. An impressive new log store and dining room replaced the store that Bill Wilkinson had built in 1930. Many new tourist cabins were built, and bathrooms were added to the old cabins along the road. A new sewage system and a new water supply system were installed and R.E.A. electrical power replaced the old water-powered generator on Middle Creek. Pahaska was dramatically upgraded in a number of ways to meet the needs of the more critical and demanding postwar tourists. At the same time, Pahaska was placed in a better position to meet the competition from a multitude of new tourist resorts that began to crop up along the Cody Road.

These changes radically altered the character of Pahaska. Its rustic phase had ended. The old lodge, the original Pahaska, no longer viewed as a commercial asset, was saved from the bulldozer by its obvious historic importance. But it no longer was the centerpiece of Pahaska.

It is unfair, perhaps, to criticize an earlier generation which had not yet become sensitized to the need for historic preservation, but it is regrettable that the Club House, built at Pahaska in 1912 by Col. Cody, was not preserved. It exists today in a mutilated form with a long employee dormitory protruding from the front of it. That progress is a mixed blessing is well-illustrated in the Pahaska of today.

By the late 1930s the Wilkinsons had eliminated meal service at Pahaska Lodge and reduced the use of its guest rooms. This trend toward limited use continued under Coe management until commercial utilization of the lodge ceased altogether. The old lodge was entered into the National Register of Historic Places in 1973.

This fine old log structure, notable for its architectural excellence, as well as for its historic significance, is worthy of maintenance and rehabilitation. Its prospects for structural repair and renewal, and appreciation as a historic site, should be excellent. Its future lies in the hands of the Coe family, whose long tradition of philanthropy and public service began at the turn of the century, when William Robertson Coe came to the Cody country. The tradition has been continued and extended by a younger generation of Coes. Mrs. Henry H. R. (Peg) Coe, who, with her late husband, acquired Pahaska four decades ago, is one of Wyoming's distinguished citizens. She has received a great deal of public recognition and many rewards for her service, including the National Secretary of State Gold Medallion Award for Meritorious Service and the Westerner Award of the Old West Trail Foundation. The University of Wyoming honored her in 1984 with its Distinguished Alumni award. In 1966 she was elected to the board of the Buffalo Bill Historical Center in Cody, Wyoming, and since 1974 has served as its chairman. Mrs. Coe's finely honed appreciation of Col. Cody's place in western history, and her dedication to the preservation of his memorabilia at the Historical Center extends to the preservation of Pahaska Tepee, his famous hunting lodge and hotel.

Today, the eighty-year-old lodge rests benignly beside the Cody Road. It is a symbol of an unhurried age when guests gathered in its lobby to enjoy the simple pleasures of rest and conversation. Today, in the haunting quietness of its interiors, one can sense the talk and laughter that once rose around the roaring blaze of its great fireplace. Memories of sumptuous dinners and music and dancing crowd out the sadness of recollection.

Meanwhile, the new Pahaska continues the tradition of service to travelers on the Cody Road.

—— About the Author ——

Dr. W. Hudson Kensel is Professor of History and former chairman, Department of History, California State University, Fresno, California. His early childhood was spent at Pahaska and Cody, Wyoming, where he came to know the places and many of the people which appear in this book. He moved to the state of Washington where he completed his education earning a Ph.D. in western United States history. He has published a number of book reviews and articles on Pacific Northwest history in various professional history journals.

Notes

Chapter 1. Pahaska's Beginnings

1. "New Town of Cody Opened," *New York Times*, November 14, 1901, p. 7. George Allen Beecher, *A Bishop of the Plains* (Philadelphia: Church Historical Society, 1950), pp. 120-21.

2. "Bill Cody Guided by Walt Kepford on First Big Game Hunting Trip," *Cody Enterprise*, February 20, 1946, p. 7.

3. President Theodore Roosevelt's respect and admiration for Col. Cody are well documented in the president's published letters. See, for instance, Elting E. Morison, ed., *The Letters of Theodore Roosevelt*, Vol. 3 (8 vols; Cambridge: Harvard University Press, 1951-54), p. 41; also, consult Vol. 4, p. 732, and Vol. 5, p. 267 in this collection. Albert E. Straub, Jr., "The Oldest National Forest," *Cody Enterprise*, March 11, 1936, Sec. 3, p. 5; Beecher, pp. 123-24.

4. Lucille N. Hicks, ed., *Park County Story* (Dallas: Taylor Publishing Co., 1980), p. 260.

5. Editorial, *Wyoming Stockgrower and Farmer* (Cody), November 3, 1903, p. 5.

6. "Beautiful Views," *Wyoming Stockgrower and Farmer*, August 25, 1902, p. 4. "A Vacation," September 1, 1903, p. 5.

7. Stella A. Foote, ed., *Letters from Buffalo Bill* (Billings: Foote Publishing Co., 1954), p. 55. A. A. Anderson, *Experiences and Impressions* (Freeport, New York: Books for Libraries Press, 1970), p. 99.

8. "Wealthy Men Coming to Mountains," *Park County Enterprise*, July 26, 1911, p. 1. Bill DeMaris, telephone conversation with author, September 5, 1982.

9. Anderson, pp. 1-6; pp. 89-119.

10. *The National Cyclopaedia of American Biography.* 61 vols. (Vol. XXIX; New York: James T. White and Co., 1941), p. 21.

11. Nellie S. Yost, *Buffalo Bill* (Chicago: The Swallow Press, Inc., 1979), p. 163; pp. 170-171.

12. Ibid., p. 303. Hicks, p. 260.

13. Information from the Federal Records Center, Denver, Colorado, shows that on December 14, 1903, W. F. Cody obtained a special permit for the use of Pahaska Tepee, located in the Yellowstone Forest Reserve. This permit was renewed by Cody on July 23, 1904, and again on January 4, 1909. Randall R. Hall, Forest Supervisor, Shoshone National Forest. Letter to author, July 2, 1982.

14. Foote, p. 59. Don Russell, *The Lives and Legends of Buffalo Bill* (Norman: University of Oklahoma Press, 1960), p. 431.

15. *Wyoming Stockgrower and Farmer*, May 3, 1905, p.1; June 7, 1905, p. 1; July 19, 1905, p. 1.

16. Richard C. Overton, *Burlington Route, A History of the Burlington Lines* (New York: Alfred A. Knopf, 1965), pp.233, 241.

17. Russell, pp. 84-85. Foote, p. 9.

18. Lucille N. Patrick (Hicks), *The Best Little Town by a Dam Site, or Cody's First 20 Years* (Cheyenne: Flintlock Publishing Co., 1968), p. 21. Charles H. Morrill, *The Morrills and Reminiscences* (Chicago: University Publishing Co., 1918). For information relating to the plotting of the Cody town site see the Lincoln Land Company Town Files in the Nebraska State Historical Society, Lincoln, Nebraska. Materials dealing with some arrangements between W. F. Cody and the Lincoln Land Company were received from the personal files of Dorrina Turner Damico. For a scholarly account of early Cody, see James D. McLaird, "Building the Town of Cody: George T. Beck, 1894-1943," *Annals of Wyoming*, (Vol. 40, April 1968). For competent studies of the Big Horn Basin, consult David J. Wasden, *From Beaver to Oil* (Cheyenne: Pioneer Printing and Stationery Co., 1973), and Charles Lindsay, *The Big Horn Basin*. University Studies of the University of Nebraska, Vols. XXVIII-XXIX (Lincoln: University of Nebraska Press, 1932).

19. The first advertisement for Pahaska appeared in the *Wyoming Stockgrower and Farmer*, June 14, 1906, p. 4.

Chapter 2. The Cody Road

1. Hiram M. Chittenden, "Improvement of the Yellowstone National Park, Including the Construction, Repair and Maintenance of Roads and Bridges," *Annual Report of the Chief of Engineers, United States Army, 1900.* (Part I; Washington, D.C.: U.S. Government Printing Office, 1900), p. 717.

2. Chittenden, *Annual Report of the Chief of Engineers . . . 1901.* Appendix FFF, pp. 3780-3782; also, consult Appendix B, pp. 3793-3794 for the detailed report of S. F. Crecelius, Assistant Engineer.

3. Chittenden, *Annual Report of the Chief of Engineers . . . 1903.* Appendix BBB, pp. 2445, 2468.

4. Chittenden, *Annual Report of the Chief of Engineers . . . 1904,* p. 738. Aubrey L. Haines, *The Yellowstone Story, A History of Our First National Park.* Vol. II (Yellowstone National Park: Yellowstone Library and Museum Association, 1977), p. 244.

5. *Park County Enterprise,* December 16, 1911, p. 2, from the *Cody Enterprise,* December, 1901.

6. *Wyoming Stockgrower and Farmer,* December 30, 1902, p. 4.

7. Ibid., July 28, 1903, p. 8.

8. Ibid., August 11, 1903, p. 8.

9. Ibid., September 1, 1903, p. 5.

10. Ibid., August 18, 1903, p. 5.

11. Dave Jones, "Cody Road Then and Now," *Cody Enterprise,* March 11, 1936, p. 1.

12. F. H. Newell, *Second Annual Report of the Reclamation Service, 1902-3* (Washington, D. C.: U. S. Government Printing Office, 1904), pp. 507-510.

13. Newell, *Third Annual Report . . . 1903-04,* pp. 630-31; *Fourth Annual Report . . . 1904-05,* p. 350.

14. Newell, *Ninth Annual Report . . . 1909-1910,* pp. 307-308, 310, 318-320. Jones, p. 1. *Wyoming Stockgrower and Farmer,* August 13, 1908, p. 1; December 10, 1908, p. 1; December 31, 1908, p. 1.

15. Lloyd M. Brett, *Report of the Acting Superintendent of the Yellowstone National Park to the Secretary of the Interior, 1911* (Washington, D.C.: U.S. Government Printing Office, 1911), p. 568. *Park County Enterprise,* October 25, 1911, p. 1.

16. Calvin W. Williams, "Seeing Wyoming From a Studebaker E.M.F. in 1909," *Annals of Wyoming,* (Vol. 51, No. 1, Spring 1979), 140.

Chapter 3. Buffalo Bill's Hotel in the Rockies

1. *Wyoming Stockgrower and Farmer,* May 31, 1905, p. 1; July 19, 1905, p. 2; August 23, 1905, p. 1.

2. Ibid., "Are You Going To The Park," June 14, 1905, p. 1; "Over the Road to Cody," July 26, 1905, p. 1; October 5, 1905, p. 5; July 11, 1907, p. 4; May 28, 1908, p. 2; July 7, 1908, p. 5; July 30, 1908, p. 5; April 1, 1909, p. 7; July 16, 1909, p. 1; July 30, 1909, p. 1. *Cody Enterprise,* May 8, 1940, pp. 1, 3.

3. *Wyoming Stockgrower and Farmer,* "Through Yellowstone National Park," May 2, 1906, p. 1.

4. Ibid.

5. *Park County Enterprise,* October 25, 1911, p. 1.

6. "The Beautiful Cody Route to the Park," *Wyoming Stockgrower and Farmer,* August 27, 1909, pp. 1, 3.

7. "The Holm Lodge is Now Open," *Park County Enterprise,* August 6, 1910, p. 5; May 4, 1910, p. 5; June 8, 1910, p. 5.

8. "Via Cody's Inns," *Wyoming Stockgrower and Farmer,* May 3, 1095, p. 1; May 17, 1905, p. 4; "Nearly Completed," May 31, 1905, p.1; "The Cody Trail," June 7, 1905, p. 1; "Going to the Park," July 19, 1905, p. 1; August 23, 1905, p. 4.

9. Ibid., February 7, 1906, p. 4; March 21, 1906, p. 4; "A Quiet Wedding," January 3, 1907, p. 4.

10. Ibid., January 7, 1909, p 6; May 27, 1909, p. 1; September 3, 1909, p. 5; September 17, 1909, p. 5. "Improvements at Pahaska," *Park County Enterprise,* June 11, 1910, p. 1; "A Big Sunday at Pahaska," July 27, 1910, p. 1.

11. "Cody Society Folks are Pahaska-Bound Saturday," *Cody Enterprise,* June 10, 1911, p. 1; "Major E. S. Hoopes Dies Following a Prolonged Illness," April 27, 1937, p. 5; *Wyoming Stockgrower and Farmer,* June 4, 1908, p. 5.

12. Glenn Shirley, *Pawnee Bill: a Biography of Major Gordon W. Lillie.* (Albuquerque: University of New Mexico Press, 1958), 196.

13. *Wyoming Stockgrower and Farmer,* "Col. Wm. F. Cody Returns from Hunt," December 3, 1909, p. 1.

14. Ibid., "Auto Scores a Success," November 26, 1909, p. 1.

15. "Automobiles for Pahaska," *Park County Enterprise*, June 4, 1910, p. 1; "Ho, for Pahaska, by Auto," June 29, 1910, p. 1; "New Chauffeur for the Irma," August 10, 1912, p. 6.

16. Ibid., June 15, 1910, p.5; July 6, 1910, p. 1; July 20, 1910, p. 4, 5.

17. Ibid., "Improvements at Pahaska," June 11, 1910, p. 1; "A Big Sunday at Pahaska," July 27, 1910, p. 1.

18. Ibid., "Jolly Pahaska Party," November 26, 1910, p. 1.

Chapter 4. Competition and Growth, 1910-1912

1. "Pahaska and Hunting Season," *Park County Enterprise*, August 24, 1910, p. 1, 4; October 1, 1910, p. 2.

2. Ibid., "Holm Buys 2 Autos for Park Trade," June 24, 1911, p. 1; "Park Traffic Warming Up," July 1, 1911, p. 2; "Holm Company Places New Stanley Car in Service," June 19, 1912, p. 2.

3. Ibid., October 25, 1911, p. 1.

4. Ibid., "All Nature Smiles as Pahaska, Gem of the Mountain Resorts, Is Thrown Open for the Season: Cody People Have Royal Time There," June 14, 1911, pp. 1, 5.

5. Ibid., p. 5.

6. Ibid.

7. Ibid., "Pahaska to Get More Amusements," June 24, 1911, p. 7.

8. Ibid., "Annual Meeting Auto Club," July 19, 1911, p. 1; "Automobile Club Visits Pahaska En Masse," August 2, 1911, p. 1.

9. Ibid., "New Car for Pahaska Trade," August 5, 1911, p. 1; "Hundred Tourists Arrive in a Single Day," August 5, 1911, p. 1; "Frost & Richard to Establish Tourist Headquarters on Robertson Ranch," November 1, 1911, p. 1; "Morris Books Large Party," May 6, 1911, p. 1.

10. Ibid., "Court Held at Pahaska," July 26, 1911, p. 1; "Eastern News Writers on Their Way to Cody," September 6, 1911, p. 1; "Mrs. Perkins at Pahaska," September 2, 1911, p. 1.

11. Ibid., "From Pahaska in 2 1/3 Hours," September 20, 1911, p. 6; "Hunting Party Near Pahaska," September 30, 1911, p. 1; "Zero Weather and Big Snow Brings Big Game Out of Mountains," November 11, 1911, p. 1.

12. Ibid., "Pahaska to Open June 8," April 10, 1912, p. 1; "Mrs. Myrtle Watkins Made Manager of Pahaska Tepee," June 5, 1912, p. 1; "Beautiful Pahaska is Opened Amid Festivities," June 12, 1912, p. 5; "Barbecue at Pahaska on July 13," July 6, 1912, p. 1. Interview with Bill DeMaris, Wyoming, April 22, 1982.

13. "Fine Club House Being Built," *Park County Enterprise*, July 17, 1912, p. 5.

14. Ibid., "Col. Cody's Daughter to Run the Irma," March 12, 1913, p. 1; March 22, 1913, p. 8; April 12, 1913, p. 8; "Reception at the Irma Hotel Tonight," April 26, 1913, p. 1.

15. Ibid., "Holm Incorporates New Tourist Company," October 28, 1911, p. 1; "Notice of Incorporation," November 8, 1911, p. 7; "Three New Autos for Holm Transportation Company," February 15, 1913, p. 1; "Pahaska to Handle Holm Transportation Co. Tourists During the Coming Season," May 17, 1913, p. 1. "Remarkable Growth—Business of Holm Transportation Co.," September 24, 1914, p. 1. Lloyd M. Brett, *Report of the Acting Superintendent of the Yellowstone National Park to the Secretary of the Interior* (Washington: Government Printing Office, 1912), pp. 641, 654.

16. "President Wiley Co. Makes Final Plans for Using the Cody Route," *Park County Enterprise*, May 1, 1912, p. 1; "Remarkable Growth—Business of the Holm Transportation Co.," September 24, 1913, p. 1.

17. Ibid., June 5, 1912, p. 1; July 3, 1912, p. 1; April 23, 1913, p. 1; "Main Building at Holm Lodge Completely Destroyed by Fire," November 15, 1913, p. 1; "Holm Lodge Purchased by Howell and Jordan Co.," May 20, 1914, p. 8.

Chapter 5. Famous Hunt and Unusual Events

1. "Large Auto Parties to Pahaska Today," *Park County Enterprise*, June 14, 1913, p. 1; "Pahaska is Opened for the Season Amid Gay Festivities of Natives," June 18, 1913, p. 1.

2. Ibid., "Pahaska to Handle Holm Transportation Co. Tourists During the Coming Season," May 17, 1913, pp. 1, 4; Clarence H. Knight, *Annual Report of the Chief of Engineers . . . 1913* (Washington, D.C.: U.S. Government Printing Office, 1913), p. 1488.

3. "Prince to Hunt Bears," *New York Times*, July 20, 1913, Pt. 3, p. 4; "Prince of Monaco Here on His Yacht," September 11, 1913, p. 3; "Prince Albert Departs," September 13, 1913, p. 6.

4. "Wild West Show Fails," *New York Times*, July 29, 1913, p.11; "Save Isham for Col. Cody," August 22, 1913, p. 1; Yost, pp.384-87.

5. Nancy M. Peterson, "Buffalo Bill, the Movie Maker," *The Denver Post*, February 7, 1977, pp.

26-33; Brian Garfield, *Western Films* (New York: Rawston Associates, 1982), pp.16-19; George N. Fenin and William K. Everson, *The Western from Silents to the Seventies* (New York: Grossman Publishers, 1973), pp. 47, 49, 53; Don Russell, "Buffalo Bill in Action," *The Westerners Brand Book* (Vol. 19, No. 5, July 1962), pp. 33-35, 40.

6. *Park County Enterprise*, September 13, 1913, p. 1.

7. "Cody Townsfolk Greet Prince With Rousing Western Welcome," *The Denver Post*, September 16, 1913, p. 18.

8. Ibid., "Monaco's Prince Says He'd Like to Be Mayor of Cody If He Didn't Have Job Ruling Monte Carlo," September 17, 1913, p. 16; *Park County Enterprise*, September 17, 1913, p. 8; Ibid., September 20, 1913, p. 1.

9. Anderson, pp. 212-214.

10. "Frontier Village of Forty Years Ago Rebuilt for Moving Pictures of Life in the Old West," *The Denver Post*, September 23, 1913, p. 3; *Park County Enterprise*, September 30, 1913, p. 1.

11. Ibid., October 1, 1913, p. 1.

12. Jack Richard, "Royalty Hunts in the Rockies," *Western Sportsman* (May, 1940), pp. 15-16, 27-29; Helene Day "En Selle Avec Buffalo Bill," *Annals Monegasques: Revue D'Historie de Monaco* (No. 8, 1984), pp. 48-59; "Gates Rushing to Join Buffalo Bill in Big Bear Hunt," *The Denver Post*, September 24, 1913, p. 2; "Spend-A-Million" Gates at Cody to Join Prince of Monaco in Hunt," September 25, p. 1; "Gates' Special Car Arrives in Cody; Waits for Prince," September 26, 1913, p. 9; "Prince of Monaco Expects First Shot at Bear and Promises Friends Steak for Supper," September 29, 1913, p. 1; " 'Twas Small Bear But Prince Shot It," *The (Chicago) Inter Ocean*, October 17, 1913, p. 5; "Return From Hunt. Go to Pine Ridge," *Park County Enterprise*, October 4, 1913, p. 1; "Geo. Richard Prepares Carcasses for Prince," October 15, 1913, p. 1; Fred Richard, "Cody Entertains the Prince of Monaco," *Cody Enterprise*, February 20, 1946, Sec. 2, p. 4; "Prince Kills an Elk," *New York Times*, October 4, 1913, p. 1; "Prince's Hunting Trip Ended," October 15, 1913, p. 17; "Carnegie is Glad Kaiser Took Pledge," October 27, 1913, p. 9; "Prince Albert of Monaco Sails," October 20, 1913, p. 9.

13. *Park County Enterprise*, March 4, 1914, p. 5; March 18, 1914, p. 1; "John 'Reckless' Davies, Pioneer Guide, Dies of Ptomaine Poisoning Monday," March 25, 1914, p. 1.

14. Ibid., "Mystery Surrounds Strange Death of Miss Edna Durell," March 25, 1914, pp. 1, 8.

15. Ibid., "Colonel Cody Leaves for Washington, D.C.," February 14, 1914, p. 1; "Pahaska Will Be Opened June 1st," May 23, 1914, pp. 1, 8; May 30, 1914, p. 5.

16. Ibid., "Wylie Transportation Company Opens Office," June 17, 1914, p. 1; August 29, 1914, p. 5.

17. Ibid., "Automobile Association Enjoys Pahaska Session," August 5, 1914, p. 1; August 29, 1914, p. 5; September 23, 1914, p. 5; "Paul C. Blum," December 23, 1914, p. 1.

Chapter 6. Autos to Yellowstone

1. Haines, p. 167. Chester A. Lindsley, *Report of the Acting Supervisor of the Yellowstone National Park to the Secretary of the Interior, 1917* (Washington, D.C.: U.S. Government Printing Office, 1917), p. 911.

2. "Volunteer Bands of Citizens Will Work on Canyon Road," *Park County Enterprise*, April 21, 1915, p. 1; "Canyon Bee Day Tomorrow—Go Volunteer to Work on Road—Tomorrow—Thursday, June 24—," June 23, 1915, p. 1; "Thirty Business Men Help Make Canyon Bee an Entire Success," June 26, 1915, p. 1.

3. Ibid., July 17, 1918, p. 1.

4. Ibid., "Park Road in Good Shape," June 16, 1920, p. 5. S. P. Van Arsdall, telephone conversation with author, May 16, 1982.

5. Lindsley, *Report of the Acting Supervisor of the Yellowstone National Park . . . 1918* (Washington, D.C.: U.S. Government Printing Office, 1918), p. 846.

6. "Canyon Creek Flood Changes Course of River. Cody Citizens and Tourists Turn Out En Masse to Repair Damaged Highway." *Cody Enterprise*, July 25, 1923, p. 1.

7. "Pahaska to Open About June First," *Park County Enterprise*, May 19, 1915, p. 1; July 24, 1915, p. 5; August 7, 1915, p. 5.

8. Ibid., "Joe Wolf and 'Kid' Wilson Get Contract," February 24, 1915, p. 8; "Wiley People Say Good Cody Business," April 24, 1915, p. 1; "Prospect Good Business Holm Transportation Co.," May 15, 1915, p. 1; "Twelve Passenger White Cars Arrive," May 19, 1915, p. 1.

9. Ibid., "Appropriation Committee Has Successful Trip Over Sylvan," July 7, 1915, p. 1.

10. Ibid., "Pahaska Will Entertain Pubic July 31," July 21, 1915, p. 1; "Historical Parade Will be

Novel Feature of Celebration That Marks Opening of Park," July 24, 1915, p. 1; "Autos Estimated Conservatively at Twenty," July 28, 1915, p. 1; August 4, 1915, p. 1.

11. Ibid., "Burlington Officials Here, and Make Statement," March 22, 1916, p. 1; "Hon. A. W. Miles, Nephew of our Gen. Miles, Visits Cody on Business," April 5, 1916, p. 1.

12. Mae Urbanek (as told by "Kid" Wilson), "First Auto Travel in Yellowstone Park," *Bits and Pieces*, II (No. 2, 1966), 21-22. Lindsley, *Report of Acting Supervisor of the Yellowstone National Park . . . 1916* (Washington, D.C.: U.S. Government Printing Office, 1916), pp. 776-777.

13. David M. Steele, *Going Abroad Overland* (New York: G.P. Putnam's Sons, 1917), pp. 112-13.

14. Ibid., pp. 122-24.

15. "M'Laughlin Ranch is Sold to New Yorkers," *Park County Enterprise*, June 5, 1915, p. 1; "Blackwater to be Opened During Winter," January 8, 1916, p. 1.

16. Lindsley, *Report of the Acting Supervisor of the Yellowstone National Park . . . 1917* (Washington, D.C.: U.S. Government Printing Office, 1917), pp. 811-13; Haines, p. 364.

17. "Contemplates Park County Investments," *Park County Enterprise*, March 20, 1915, p. 1; "May Purchase Both Irma Hotel and Pahaska Tepee," March 24, 1915, p. 1; "TE, Buffalo Bill's Home Place, to be Opened as Dude Ranch," December 29, 1915, p. 1.

18. Ibid., "Fred Garlow Makes Improvements in Hotel," June 20, 1917, p. 1; July 25, 1917, p. 8. Fred H. Garlow, interview with author, Cody, Wyoming, June 26, 1981. On October 6, 1917, the estate of Edwin Hall was issued a special permit for use of Pahaska Tepee, located in the Shoshone National Forest. Randall R. Hall, Forest Supervisor, Shoshone National Forest, letter to author, July 2, 1982.

Chapter 7. New Owners: Montanans Lulu Hall and Jack F. Files

1. Lindsley, *Report of the Acting Supervisor of the Yellowstone National Park . . . 1918* (Washington, D.C.: U.S. Government Printing Office, 1918), pp. 923-24. Background on Lulu Hall is scanty. People who knew her during the years she was around Cody, Wyoming, remember little about her. Research in the library, historical society and early newspapers of Roundup, Montana, reveal nothing about Mrs. Hall. Her grandson, Edwin L. Hall, generously supplied me with a photograph of Lulu, but he also knew little of her background.

2. *Cody Enterprise*, June 21, 1922, p. 8. Francis T. Hayden, telephone conversation with author, April 14, 1982.

3. A. R. "Brownie" Newton, interview with author, Cody, Wyoming, July 1, 1981; and telephone conversation with author, April 13, 1982.

4. "Pahaska Tepee to be Re-opened Immediately," *Park County Enterprise*, April 2, 1919, p. 5; June 11, 1919, p. 5; March 31, 1920, p. 5; April 14, 1920, p. 5; August 11, 1920, p. 5.

5. Ibid., "Biggest Day Yet At Pahaska Tepee," August 18, 1920, p. 1. Horace M. Albright, *Report of the Superintendent of the Yellowstone National Park . . .1921*, (Washington, D.C.: U.S. Government Printing Office, 1921), p. 156; Report . . . 1924, p. 95.

6. *Park County Enterprise*, October 13, 1920, p. 8; March 23, 1921, p. 8.

7. Ibid., "Things Will Be Doing at Pahaska Tepee," January 26, 1921, p. 1; June 15, 1921, p. 8; June 22, 1921, p. 8; July 6, 1921, p. 8; "Party at Pahaska Ends in Park Tour," July 20, 1921, p. 1. Mrs. Alice Donnell, telephone conversation with author, March 30 and April 16, 1982.

8. *The Midwest Review*, VIII (March, 1927), 96. *Park County Enterprise*, April 6, 1921, p. 8; August 24, 1921, p. 8. *Cody Enterprise*, March 1, 1922, p. 8; May 10, 1922, p. 8; June 14, 1922, p. 8; October 24, 1923, p. 8; May 21, 1924, p. 8.

9. *Park County Enterprise*, November 16, 1921, p. 8; *Cody Enterprise*, June 7, 1922, p. 8; August 1, 1923, p. 5; September 12, 1923, p. 8; October 24, 1923, p. 8; "Alex Chapaton Dies in Detroit Hospital," December 12, 1923, p. 1.

10. Ibid., "Dayer Resigns Irma Management," January 25, 1922, p. 1; "Cody Entrance to Park Leads Them All in Automobile Travel," October 18, 1922, p. 1; "17,644 Tourists Through Park," July 18, 1923, p. 4; "Some 43,354 Tourists Are Estimated to Have Visited Yellowstone by Cody Way," September 12, 1923, p. 4; "Gov. and Mrs. Ross Like Pahaska Tepee," September 19, 1923, p.3.

11. Ibid., "J. F. Files Buys Pahaska Tepee from Hall Estate," January 16, 1924, p. 1; "Mrs. Lulu Hall Dies May 26 in California," June 13, 1928, p. 6. Mrs. Hall's obituary appeared in the *Los Angeles Times*, May 30, 1928, Pt. 1, p. 20. Fred H. Garlow, interview with author, June 26, 1982.

12. "J. F. Files To Be Manager Irma Cafe," *Cody Enterprise*, February 20, 1924, p. 1; "John F. Files Answers Death's Call," February 23, 1925, p. 1.

Chapter 8. The Bizarre Case of Roscoe F. Warren

1. "Pahaska Bought by Members Mutual Rocky Mountain Club," *Cody Enterprise*, May 14, 1924, p. 1. For various newspaper reports on Roscoe Warren's early activities in the Cody County, see *Park County Enterprise*, May 4, 1921, p. 8; July 27, 1921, p. 8; November 9, 1921, p. 8. *Cody Enterprise*, November 7, 1923, p. 1; December 5, 1923, p. 8.

2. Ibid., June 18, 1924, p. 8; "Medical and Dental Meetings Come to a Successful Close," June 25, 1924, p. 1.

3. Ray Prante, telephone conversation with author, April 13, 1982.

4. "Owner of Pahaska Shoots Up Meeting," *Cody Enterprise*, October 15, 1924, p. 1. "Pahaska Man Kills at K. C.," *Park County Herald*, October 15, 1924, p. 1. "Fear J. C. Deskin Will Die," *Kansas City Times*, October 14, 1924, p. 2.

5. "Deskin's Condition is Same," *Kansas City Times*, October 15, 1924, p. 3; "No Visitors for Warren," October 17, 1924, p. 1; "Funeral Notices," October 17, 1924, p. 16.

6. Ibid., "A Charge For Warren," October 21, 1924, p. 3; "Warren Is Held For Murder," November 1, 1924, p. 2; "Warren Trial Started in Kansas City Monday," *Park County Herald*, May 6, 1925, p. 1.

7. Ibid., "Roscoe F. Warren Married at K.C.," February 3, 1926, p. 1. "Warren on Trial for Murder of K.C. Man," *Cody Enterprise*, February 1, 1928, p. 7; "Warren Must Hang Says a K.C. Jury," April 4, 1928, p. 1; "Missouri Court Sentences Warren to Hang June First," May 2, 1928, p. 2; "Warren Gets a New Trial in Kansas City," June 18, 1930, p. 1; "Roscoe Warren to Serve Term for Slaying of Deskin," February 18, 1931, p. 5; "Roscoe Warren K.C. Killer a Free Man," June 27, 1934, p. 8.

8. Frank A. Arnold, Grand Secretary, Grand Lodge A.F. and A.M. of Missouri, letter to author, May 10, 1982.

9. Merna C. Miller, telephone conversations with author, April 14, 15 and 20, 1982; and interview with author, Fresno, California, June 8, 1982.

10. Records Section, County Clerk's Office, Park County Courthouse, Cody, Wyoming. Affidavit by J. Burton Warren and Bill of Sale from Roscoe F. Warren to Donald B. Warren, Book 61, p. 293.

Chapter 9. Wilkinson Era Begins, 1925.

1. Department of Records, Jackson County Courthouse, Kansas City, Missouri. Articles of Incorporation of the Wymozoca Realty Company, Book 2495, pp. 619-21, Instrument No. 202416.

2. Jessie B. Kensel, telephone conversation with author, March 25 and April 22, 1982.

3. "J. B. Warren Arrives to Open Pahaska Tepee," *Cody Enterprise*, May 6, 1925, p. 1; "New Manager is Here to Take Over Pahaska," May 20, 1925, p. 1. "D. R. Nuss to Have Charge Pahaska Tepee," *Park County Herald*, May 20, 1925, p. 1; June 10, 1925, p. 1.

4. County Clerk's Office, Park County, Wyoming. Bill of Sale from J. Burton Warren and Donald B. Warren to the Wymozoca Realty Company, Book 30, p. 265-67.

5. Jessie B. Kensel, interview with author, Bellevue, Washington, June 15, 1982.

6. Albright, *Report of the Superintendent of the Yellowstone Park . . . 1924* (Washington, D.C.: U.S. Government Printing Office, 1924), p. 95. "Dedication Services for New Road and Bridge Held in Canyon Sunday," *Cody Enterprise*, June 24, 1925, p. 1; "Yellowstone 1926 Season Smashes Previous Motor Travel Records," October 20, 1926, p. 1; "Shoshone Canyon Road Opened to Travel," February 2, 1927, p. 1; "Tourists in Parade On Way to Park," June 3, 1931, p. 1.

7. Ibid., "Pete Nordquist Buys the Majo at Valley," February 19, 1930, p. 1; "Notice of Incorporation of Four Bear Ranch Company," March 5, 1930, p. 4; "Wilkinsons Back," April 30, 1930, p. 1; "Blackwater Camp Bot by Tex Wisdom," May 14, 1930, p. 4; "New Elephant Head Building Finished," June 4, 1930, p. 1; "Earl Hayner Returns to Ranch on Northfork," April 15, 1931, p. 1; *The Midwest Review*, pp.1-3. For an account of life at Holm Lodge during the 1920s and 1930s see Mary Shawver, *Sincerely, Mary S.*, (Casper: Prairie Publishing Co., n.d.)

8. S. P. Van Arsdall, telephone conversations with author, May 16, 1982. *Cody Enterprise*, November 21, 1923, p. 8.

9. "New Sewage System Installed at Pahaska," *Park County Herald*, June 17, 1925, p. 4; May 19, 1926, p. 8.

10. S. P. Van Arsdall, telephone conversation with author, May 16, 1982; and interview with author, Cody, Wyoming, July 30, 1982. Clytie Williams, interview with author, Cody, Wyoming, July 29, 1982.

11. Jessie B. Kensel, interview with author, Bellevue, Washington, July 15, 1982. "Nuss To Be Instructor in Oklahoma Hi School," *Cody Enterprise*, August 31, 1927, p. 6; "Dale Nuss Here With Boys for Park Trip," June 20, 1928, p. 1; July 3, 1929, p. 12; July 9, 1930, p. 10; "Dale Nuss With Boys Party Here," July 1, 1931, p. 5. "Dude Party Arrives from Okmulgee, Okla.," June 29, 1932,

p. 1; "Nuss Brings Party from Southland," July 12, 1933, p. 1; July 11, 1934, p. 4; August 21, 1935, p. 8; July 6, 1938, p. 8.

12. Ibid., "Starts From Valley Biggest Pack Trip," July 4, 1923, p. 3; "Valley Ranch's Big Parties Return Delighted With Trip," August 22, 1923, p. 5; "Valley Parties Finish Trip—Return to East," August 18, 1926, p. 1; "Valley Ranch Parties Arrive on 4th and 5th," July 6, 1927, p. 1; "President of Valley Ranch Anticipates Banner Season," July 3, 1929, p. 1; "Many Dudes Arrive at Valley Ranch," July 2, 1930, p. 1.

Chapter 10. Pahaska in the 1930s.
1. Edith Baker Kemp, telephone conversation with author, March 28, 1982. Leo F. Urban, telephone conversation with author, March 28, 1982. Merle Spencer, telephone conversation with author, March 28, 1982.

2. Clytie Williams, interview with author, Cody, Wyoming, July 29, 1982. Fred H. Garlow, interview with author, Cody, Wyoming, July 29, 1982.

3. Clytie Williams, telephone conversation with author, April 17, 1982. Edith Baker Kemp, telephone conversation with author, March 28, 1982.

4. *Cody Enterprise*, May 12, 1926, p. 8; May 25, 1927, p. 10.

5. Melvin C. McGee, telephone conversation with author, April 17, 1982.

6. "Bad Bears Departed From Park, Raise Ned at Northfork Ranches," *Cody Enterprise*, August 31, 1938, pp. 1, 8.

7. Ibid.

8. Clytie Williams, telephone conversation with author, April 17, 1982.

9. "Carl Wagoner's Death Shocks Many Friends" *Cody Enterprise*, September 26, 1934, p. 8.

10. Ibid., "This Season Will Break All Yellowstone Travel Records," August 21, 1929, p. 1; September 12, 1934, p. 1; "Park Tourists Travel Makes Banner Year," September 19, 1934, p. 1; "Yellowstone Park Travel Less Than Half of 1941, Chart Shows," September 16, 1942, p. 1.

11. Ibid., "Managers Back to Holm Lodge for New 1933 Season," Apri *1933, p. 1. Clytie Williams, telephone conversation with author, April 17, 1982.*

12. "Comparative Travel Figures Show Decreased Park Travel," Cody Enterprise, July 13, 1932, p. 1; "Travel To Yellowstone Park Is Lower Compared Last Year," July 12, 1933, p. 1; September 12, 1934, p. 1.

Chapter 11. An Era of Transition, 1939-1946
1. *Cody Enterprise*, September 3, 1937, p. 1; September 15, 1937, p. 1.

2. Ibid., "Codyites Tour Northfork to Find Area for Winter Sports," January 11, 1939, p. 1.

3. Ibid., "Dahlems Plan Winter Sports Carnival at Red Star Camp," February 1, 1939, p. 1.

4. Ibid., "Ski Club Decides to Run One Up-ski at Red Star Camp," September 20, 1939, p. 1; "20 Gilded Bedsteads Reposing in Pahaska Ski-Lodge Foundation," October 4, 1939, p. 1; "New Ski-Tow Almost Complete at Pahaska," January 3, 1940, p. 1; "Mountains Crowded by Skiers Although Snow Disappointing," January 10, 1940, p. 1. "Wintersports Snow Still Below Normal, Many Enjoy Skiing," January 17, 1940, p. 1.

5. Ibid., "Fifty Thousand Dollar Lodge at Pahaska to Open on Sunday," November 20, 1940, p. 1; "Ski Club Plans 1st Dance New Pahaska Tepee Lodge," December 4, 1940, p. 1.

6. Ibid., "55 Use Ski-Lift at Pahaska Sun.; Falls Convulse Non-Skiers," January 29, 1941, p. 1; "400 Gather to Ski and Watch Skiing at Pahaska Tepee," February 5, 1941, p. 1; "Huge Crowd Turns Out for Ski Meet Here Sunday; Hansen Wins," February 26, 1941, p. 1.

7. Ibid., "Work Commences on Northfork Ski Run," August 27,1941, p. 4; "Opening of Ski Season Planned New Year's Upper Northfork," December 31, 1941, p. 1; "Work is Rushed on New Ski Course Tow," January 7, 1942, p. 8; "Billings Skiers Assist Locals in Opening Course," January 28, 1942, p. 1; "Annual Ski Meet Sunday at Pahaska and Sleeping Giant," February 11, 1942, p. 1

8. Haines, p. 479.

9. "Pahaska Tepee's New Hunting, Ski Lodge Destroyed in $75,000 Blaze Friday Night," *Cody Enterprise*, September 16, 1942 p. 1. Tom F. Trimmer, telephone conversation with author, April 17,1982.

10. "East Entrance Y.N.P. Open to Travel May 30," *Cody Enterprise*, May 24, 1944, p. 4; "Yellowstone Park Travel Increases," October 18, 1944, p. 8; "Yellowstone Park to Officially Close September 4th—Limited Service in Park Until October 1st," August 29, 1945, p. 1.

11. Ibid., "Northfork Skiers Report Good Snow," December 5, 1945, p. 1; "Pahaska Tepee

Share Bought By Henry Coe," April 10, 1946, p. 1; "Pahaska Interests Now Owned by Coe," October 9, 1946, p. 1. Records Section, County Clerk's Office, Park County, Wyoming. Bill of Sale for an Undivided 7/10th or Seventy Percent Interest from Alberta E. Wilkinson to Henry H. R. Coe, Book 107, p. 118. Ibid., Bill of Sale for an Undivided 3/10th or Thirty Percent Interest from Alberta E. Wilkinson to Pahaska Company, Book 107, p. 121.

Bibliography

Books, Magazine Articles, Newspapers and Published Documents

Albright, Horace M. *Report of the Superintendent of the Yellowstone National Park to the Secretary of the Interior, 1921.* Washington, D.C.: U.S. Government Printing Office, 1921.

—. *Report of the Superintendent of the Yellowstone National Park to the Secretary of the Interior, 1924.* Washington, D.C.: U.S. Government Printing Office, 1924.

Anderson, A.A. *Experiences and Impressions.* Freeport, New York: Books for Libraries Press, 1970.

Beecher, George Allen. *A Bishop of the Great Plains.* Philadelphia: Church Historical Society, 1950.

Brett, Lloyd M. *Report of the Acting Superintendent of the Yellowstone National Park to the Secretary of the Interior, 1911.* Washington, D.C.: U.S. Government Printing Office, 1911.

—. *Report of the Acting Superintendent of the Yellowstone National Park to the Secretary of the Interior, 1912.* Washington, D.C.: U.S. Government Printing Office, 1912.

The (Chicago) Inter Ocean, 1913.

Chittenden, Hiram M. "Improvement of the Yellowstone National Park, Including the Construction, Repair and Maintenance of Roads and Bridges." *Annual Report of the Chief of Engineers, United States Army, 1900.* Part 1. Washington, D.C.: U.S. Government Printing Office, 1900.

—. "Improvement of the Yellowstone National Park, Including the Construction, Repair and Maintenance of Roads and Bridges." *Annual Report of the Chief of Engineers, United States Army, 1901.* Appendix FFF and B. Washington, D.C.: U.S. Government Printing Office, 1901.

—. "Improvement of the Yellowstone National Park, Including the Construction, Repair and Maintenance of Roads and Bridges," *Annual Report of the Chief of Engineers, United States Army, 1903.* Appendix BBB. Washington, D.C.: U.S. Government Printing Office, 1903.

—"Improvement of the Yellowstone National Park, Including the Construction, Repair and Maintenance of Roads and Bridges" *Annual Report of the Chief of Engineers, United States Army, 1904.* Appendix FFF. Washington, D.C.: U.S. Government Printing Office, 1904.

The Cody Enterprise, 1901, 1910-1911, 1921-1925, 1928-1946.

The Cody Enterprise and the *Park County Herald,* 1926-1927.

Day, Helene. "En Selle Avec Buffalo Bill." Annales Monegasques: Revue d'Histoirie de Monaco. Publication des Archive Du Palais Princier. Numero 8, 1984.

The Denver Post, 1913.

Fenin, George N. and Everson, William K. *The Western From Silents to the Seventies.* New York: Grossman Publishers, 1973.

Foote, Stella A., ed. *Letters from Buffalo Bill.* Billings: Foote Publishing Co., 1954.

Garfield, Brian. *Western Films.* New York: Rawson Associates, 1982.

Haines, Aubrey L. *The Yellowstone Story, A History of Our First National Park.* Yellowstone National Park: Yellowstone Library and Museum Association, 1977.

Hicks, Lucille N., ed. *Park County Story.* Dallas: Taylor Publishing Co., 1980.

The Kansas City Times, 1924.

Knight, Clarence H. "Improvement of Yellowstone National Park, Including the Construction, Repair and Maintenance of Roads and Bridges." *Annual Report of the Chief of Engineers, United States Army, 1913.* Washington, D.C.: U.S. Government Printing Office, 1913.

Lindsley, Chester A. *Report of the Acting Supervisor of the Yellowstone National Park to the Secretary of the Interior, 1916.* Washington, D.C.: U.S. Government Printing Office, 1916.

—. *Report of the Acting Supervisor of the Yellowstone National Park to the Secretary of the*

Interior, 1917. Washington, D.C.: U.S. Government Printing Office, 1917.
—. *Report of the Acting Supervisor of the Yellowstone National Park to the Secretary of the Interior, 1918.* Washington, D.C.: U.S. Government Printing Office, 1918.
Los Angeles Times, 1928.
McLaird, James D. "Building the Town of Cody: George T. Beck, 1894-1943." *Annals of Wyoming* Vol. 40, April 1968.
The Midwest Review, VIII. March, 1972.
Morison, Elting E., ed. *The Letters of Theodore Roosevelt.* 8 vols. Cambridge: Harvard University Press, 1951-54.
Morrill, Charles H. *The Morrills and Reminiscences.* Chicago: University Publishing Co., 1918.
The National Cyclopaedia of American Biography. 61 vols. New York: James T. White and Co., 1941.
The New York Times, 1901, 1913.
Newell, F. H. *Second Annual Report of the Reclamation Service, 1902-3.* Washington, D.C.: U.S. Government Printing Office, 1904.
—. *Third Annual Report of the Reclamation Service, 1903-04.* Washington, D.C.: U.S. Government Printing Office, 1906.
—. *Fourth Annual Report of the Reclamation Service, 1904-05.* Washington, D.C.: U.S. Government Printing Office, 1906.
—. *Ninth Annual Report of the Reclamation Service, 1909-1910.* Washington, D.C.: U.S. Government Printing Office, 1911.
Overton, Richard C. *Burlington Route: A History of the Burlington Lines.* New York: Alfred A. Knopf, 1965.
Park County Enterprise, 1910-1921.
Park County Herald, 1924-1925.
Patrick, Lucille N. *The Best Little Town by a Dam Site or Cody's First 20 Years.* Cheyenne: Flintlock Publishing Co., 1968.
Richard, Jack. "Royalty Hunts in the Rockies." *Western Sportsman*, May, 1940.
Russell, Don. *The Lives and Legends of Buffalo Bill.* Norman: University of Oklahoma Press, 1960.
—. "Buffalo Bill In Action," *The Westerners Brand Book*, Vol.19, No. 5, July, 1962.
Shawver, Mary. *Sincerely, Mary S.* Casper: Prairie Publishing Co., n.d.
Shirley, Glenn. *Pawnee Bill: A Biography of Major Gordon W. Lillie.* Albuquerque: University of New Mexico Press, 1958.
Steele, David M. *Going Abroad Overland.* New York: G. P. Putnam's Sons, 1917.
Urbanek, Mae (as told by "Kid" Wilson). "First Auto Travel in Yellowstone Park." *Bits and Pieces.* II. No. 2, 1966.
Wasden, David J. *From Beaver to Oil: A Century in the Development of Wyoming's Big Horn Basin.* Cheyenne: Pioneer Printing and Stationery Co., 1973.
Williams, Calvin W. "Seeing Wyoming From A Studebaker E.M.F. in 1909," *Annals of Wyoming*, Vol. 51, Spring 1979.
Wyoming Stockgrower and Farmer, 1902-1909.
Yost, Nellie S. *Buffalo Bill.* Chicago: The Swallow Press, Inc., 1979.

Unpublished Materials.
Alston, Jessie F. Telephone conversation with author, April 16, 1982.
Arnold, Frank A. Grand Secretary, Grand Lodge A.F. and A.M. of Missouri. Letter to author, May 10, 1982.
Black, Valerie. Librarian. Yellowstone Library and Museum Association. Letter to author, May 20, 1982.
Borron, Hulda, Telephone conversation with author, April 14, 1982.
Braden, Leatha. Interview with author, Fresno, California, June 8, 1982.
—. Telephone conversation with author, April 14 and 20, 1982.
Brown, Hugh. Telephone conversation with author, April 13 1982.
Damico, Darrina Turner. Letter to author, July 25, 1982.
DeMaris, Bill. Telephone conversation with the author, April 22, 1982 and September 5, 1982.
Donnell, Alice F. Letter to author, April 29, 1982.
—. Telephone conversation with author, March 30, 1982 and April 16, 1982.
Garlow, Fred H. Interview with author. Cody, Wyoming, June 26, 1981 and July 29, 1982.
—. Telephone conversation with author, April 27, 1982.

Haines, Aubrey L. Letter to author, May 18, 1982.

Hall, Randall R., Forest Supervisor, Shoshone National Forest. Letter to author, July 2, 1982.

Hayden, Francis T. Telephone conversation with author, April 14, 1982.

Hicks, Lucille Nichols. Letters to author, April 7, 1982; May 14, 1982.

—. Telephone conversation with author, March 24, 1982.

Kemp, Edith Baker. Letters to author, April 6, 1982; May 19, 1982.

 —. Telephone conversation with author, March 28, 1982.

Kensel, Jessie B. Interview with author, Bellevue, Washington, June 3 and 15, 1982; July 15, 1982.

—. Telephone conversation with author, March 25, 1982 and April 22, 1982.

Larson, Grace Files. Interview with author, Cody, Wyoming, July 1, 1981.

McGee, Melvin C. Telephone conversation with author, April 17, 1982.

Madsen, Carl W. Letter to author, April 28, 1982.

—. Telephone conversation with author, March 30, 1982.

Miller, Merna C. Letters to author, April 28, 1982, May 24, 1982.

—. Interview with author. Fresno, California, June 8, 1982.

—. Telephone conversation with author, April 14, 15, and 20, 1982.

Missouri. Jackson County. Department of Records. "Articles of Incorporation of the Wymozoca Realty Company." Book 2495, pp. 619-21. Instrument No. 202416.

Newton, A. R. "Brownie." Interview with author, Cody, Wyoming, July 1, 1981.

—. Telephone conversation with author, April 13, 1982.

Osborne, Sam. Interview with author, Cody, Wyoming, July 28, 1982.

—. Telephone conversation with author, March 23, 1982.

Overton, Richard C. Letter to author, May 26, 1982.

Paul, Andrea I. Manuscripts Curator. Nebraska State Historical Society. Letter to author, June 8, 1982.

Pierce, Marion W. Deputy County Clerk, Park County, Wyoming. Letter to author, April 28, 1982.

Prante, Ray. Telephone conversation with author, April 13, 1982.

Spencer, Merle. Telephone conversation with author, March 28, 1982.

Trimmer, Tom F. Telephone conversation with author, April 17, 1982.

Urban, Leo F. Telephone conversation with author, March 28, 1982.

Van Arsdall, S. P. Interview with author, Cody, Wyoming, July 30, 1982.

—. Telephone conversation with author, May 16, 1982.

Williams, Clytie. Interview with author, Cody, Wyoming, June 25 and 26, 1981; July 28 and 29, 1982.

—. Letter to author, May 29, 1982.

—. Telephone conversation with author, April 17, 1982.

Wyoming. Park County. Records Section. "Affidavit by J. Burton Warren and Bill of Sale from Roscoe F. Warren to Donald B. Warren." Book 61, p. 293.

—. Park County. Records Section. "Bill of Sale from Wymozoca Realty Company to Alberta E. Wilkinson Covering All Property and Premises Known as 'Chapaton Cabin'." Book 30, p. 345.

—. Park County. Records Section. "Mortgagee's Affidavit of Sale of Personal Property from Ernest J. Goppert to Alberta E. Wilkinson." Book 61, p. 610.

—. Park County. Records Section. "Bill of Sale from J. Burton Warren and Donald B. Warren to the Wymozoca Realty Company." Book 30, pp. 265-67.

—. Park County. Records Section. "Bill of Sale for an Undivided 7/10ths or Seventy Percent Interest from Alberta E. Wilkinson to Henry H. R. Coe." Book 107, p. 118.

—. Park County. Records Section. "Bill of Sale for an Undivided 3/10ths or Thirty Percent Interest from Alberta E. Wilkinson to Pahaska Company." Book 107, p. 121.

Index